BEATING
THE FORCE OF
AVERAGE

JASON GELIOS

Published by Jason Gelios, IngramSpark and CreateSpace

ISBN 979-8-218-08211-6

Proudly printed in the USA

Cover and interior design by Jason Gelios
Cover illustration by Haley Gelios
Proofread and edited by Patricia Gordon
Photo Credit: Jeffrey Steiger

For business inquiries or multiple copy deals, please visit:
www.JasonGelios.com

For real estate inquiries, please visit:
www.ItsAllAboutTheRealEstate.com

This book is dedicated to
my two amazing children,
I am blessed to have great children
with great minds doing great things.

You inspire me daily!

CONTENTS

"Success to me means waking up almost daily not being bothered by what you don't want to do"

- Jason Gelios

WHY DO SO MANY PEOPLE SETTLE FOR AVERAGE?

Are you a victim of the *force of average?*

I would like to share with you a great scenario about an elephant and a spike. In an effort to train a baby elephant, the trainer would tie a rope around one of the baby elephant's legs, with the other end of the rope leading to a spike in the ground. This was so the baby elephant would not break free, as they were training it. As the rope was applied to the baby elephant's leg and spike, the baby elephant would try it's hardest to break free, never succeeding.

Because a baby elephant is small in size, it eventually gives up. As a baby elephant grows into a gigantic adult large in size with the strength to match, the trainer applies the same type of rope to the adult elephant's leg and spike. The adult elephant remembers the rope and spike, and never tries to break free, because it hasn't had luck doing so in the past. Therefore, the elephant never really tries to free itself from the spike. If the adult elephant only knew that it could easily break free from the spike, the elephant would realize it could set itself free. The elephant lives the rest of its life under what we call the *force of average*.

When you hear someone say the word average, what comes to mind? Do you envision someone settling for less? Is it someone who does just enough to get by? Could it be that you're the one settling for an average life that you don't care for? Do you feel that the things in your life are average or that something is missing? Do you lack the ambition or drive to do the work that you currently are doing daily, feeling unmotivated to pursue your passion?

If you, or someone you know, are waking up dreading the day without any excitement to create and seize opportunity, then you might be held down by what is called the *force of average*. I don't think anybody goes about looking to be average in what they do. Could you imagine if that was someone's goal every day? To go out into the world and underachieve at everything they come across. Believe it or not, many people are like the elephant tied to the spike that I mentioned earlier.

At some point in our life, we all have been faced with the *force of average*. We become content with doing average work while others are achieving the things they want out of life, or the things we want out of life. It may seem as though happy and successful people always make the right decisions to get all the breaks in life. Successful people are so damn lucky to be alive! We tell ourselves that we can't have the same luck as them because it's just not meant for us. We might tell ourselves that we're not smart enough, or we lack the talent to be a success in our life. Maybe we listen to those around us telling us that we should just be happy with what we have. Just like the elephant and the spike scenario I shared with you, we settle for average and think we can't break free.

I know, from my own life experiences, how it feels to dread going to work for a job I hate, while consistently thinking about time spent outside of work. I know what it's like to not be passionate about what I was doing. You can ask anybody who has known me for a while, I bounced around from job to job trying to find something I didn't mind doing. The problem with this method was that every job I was qualified for was the same routine. I soon realized that nothing big was going to happen unless I made a big change in myself.

When I was younger, my time was spent accepting the *force of average* and living in an average routine. I felt it was my destiny to just get by in life with the work I was doing at the time, and that I wasn't meant for great things. I almost fell completely victim to the *force of average* when suddenly it hit me.

One day I decided that I had enough. I was fed up with where I was at in life and I knew that I had to do something to change the path I was on. I embraced a change in my mindset and applied all the tips I share in this book to create a life that I truly wanted to live, allowing me to overcome the *force of average* for myself. Once I figured out what I wanted to do and sought out the necessary education to be the person I wanted to be, I saw a better version of myself forming.

Maybe the title caught your attention and you are curious about what the *force of average* is and whether or not it's being applied to your life in some way shape or form. You may feel stuck where you're at, living an average life, feeling like you're going nowhere without any resolve.

In this book, you will learn what the *force of average* is and how to beat it. You will gain real world knowledge that can be applied to your daily routine so that you can get going and change the direction of your sail to achieve the success you desire. For me, when I learned and applied these principles, endless opportunities came my way, because I learned how to look for them. I learned how to recognize opportunities that would lead to me creating better life for myself.

By the time you are finished reading this book, you will have all the necessary tools and information to make that positive change in your life. You will be an unstoppable force-achieving success along the way.

There is one catch though.

You have to want to do it.

You see, you can gain all the information in the world, but if it's not applied to what you are trying to do, nothing will happen. No positive change. No success. No nothing. Well, a whole lot of nothing! You will have succumbed to the *force of average* and remain stagnant where your feet are currently planted. And that's no good.

In this book I share success stories of others who have beaten the *force of average* to overcome the challenges that were placed in front of them so that they could achieve great things in their life. They share ways of getting through challenges and how they created a life filled with purpose and fulfillment.

If you are interested in learning what the *force of average* is and how you can beat it for your better good, then it's time to read further on.

-Jason Gelios

What is the *Force of Average?*

You may not know what the *force of average* is or how it can affect our daily lives. Chances are you haven't heard about the *force of average* prior to picking up this book. If you were to search online for more information on the *force of average*, you would find many references to mathematical equations and other information that doesn't pertain to us changing our lives. I guarantee we won't be covering any mathematical formulas in this book. Plus I stink at math!

While you may have just learned about the *force of average*, I'd like to think that almost everyone knows what average actually looks like. Average is the job or boss we hate as we daydream of a vacation away from it all. Average is the life that is boring, uneventful and mundane, especially when compared to others who seem to have it all. It's that very moment where we feel as though we don't deserve more than what we have because we think we are not smart enough to go after it. Therefore, we stay in one spot for the rest of our lives, settling for less, under the *force of average*.

So how does the *force of average* get thrown into our daily lives?

The *force of average* is instilled upon many of us as a way to have us think that it's impossible to be successful in our own life. Its main objective is to make us feel that we are destined to be average and that we must settle for less in life. This force applies the thinking that we shouldn't go after our dreams because we won't get there anyway. The *force of average* will fill our minds with self doubt, indecisiveness and even a lack of courage.

As I mentioned earlier, we won't be talking about the *force of average* as it applies to mathematics. Instead, we will be talking about how the *force of average* applies itself to your life and how you can beat it; allowing you to lead a life on your own terms. This book is for those who are not where they want to be, living a life they dread. Maybe you know someone who falls under this description. Maybe I just described you. If that's the case, then you have the right information in your hands.

So what exactly makes me an expert on this topic?

I know first-hand what it's like to fall victim to the *force of average*. I was working in countless dead end jobs, hating every day of the week, while anticipating the weekend's arrival. I was the guy who couldn't wait for a day off. I've worked for bosses that I couldn't stand, watched as others around me were working for more money with less back breaking labor, and dealt with the mentality of average thinking. I hated feeling like I was just getting by with mediocre pay and no real opportunity. It just doesn't feel right to live life this way! While I was grateful for the good things I had, such as great parents and people around me, I wanted more out of life. I was sick and tired of being sick and tired.

Many of us, at birth, are destined to live an average life. I know this sounds profound but it's true. As we go through life, society tries to tempt us with so many distractions that can keep us from success. Whether its binge watching useless television shows to getting involved in someone's drama or gossip, these time suck activities can keep us in an average lifestyle. I've seen too many people complain about how awful their life is, claiming they don't have time to make a change for the better, only to never change the direction of their life.

Sure they can tell you what happened in the latest television show or what new drama surfaced about others. People who complain consistently about their life lose the right to share their complaints with others, because they can make the change, and they don't. They made a choice to stay where they are at; under the *force of average*.

And they will bring you down too, if you let them.

Being under the *force of average* will:

- rob you of your true potential

- provide you with all kinds of excuses as to why you won't do something

- make procrastination and flat out laziness a priority

- keep you in your current situation and state of mind

- want you to accept average and think that you can't do the great things you want to do

Let's clarify what I'm saying here.

If you're perfectly fine living an average life and you don't want to make a change to achieve the success you desire, then this is where you put this book down. It would be my guess, though, that if you were that type of person, you would not be reading this book. You know you are different. You know you are tired of the status quo.

You know you want to make a positive change in your life and set a course towards a new direction towards a new life. You might currently hate your job, boss or even your co-workers. It's safe to say that most do. You may hate the pay you get or feel that you aren't getting anywhere doing what you're currently doing. Most do. I'm here to tell you that your life does not have to be this way! You have a choice.

When you realize that you can beat the *force of average* and achieve so much more out of life by adjusting your sail, you can head towards a life of happiness and success.

Like I said, I have been in that position where I hated what I was doing. Every day was hell for me, working towards what felt like nothing important. It wasn't until I set my trajectory in another direction that I really started to see change in my life. When I applied the tips I share in this book to my life, I saw positive changes start to happen. And I have never looked back.

Let's dive deeper into the five things I shared earlier about what the *force of average* will do.

ONE: The *Force Of Average* will rob you of your true potential

Not only will the *force of average* try to keep you in a life you don't look forward to, it will make it seem impossible to go after what you really want. When one person tells another person that what they want to do is too hard and it probably won't work out. Then you have the naysayers, the doubters, the know-it-all's who all think that they are protecting you from failure by telling you something won't work out. You may know one or more of these types of people. They may think they are helping you, but they really aren't doing you any favors.

If you allow these types of people or things to interfere with your new found thinking, it will rob you of your true potential. Hearing advice from someone who has never done what you are about to do is detrimental to you becoming successful.

TWO: The *force of average* provides you with all kinds of excuses as to why you won't do something

There are all kinds of excuses as to why we shouldn't do something different or new. When we think of something we want to do, we will run scenarios through our head of what could go wrong if we tried something different. A sort of fear paralysis kicks in keeping us from actually moving forward on the thing we are considering doing. We may even get scared of what others will think if we do end up trying something new and failing at it.

Our brain is wired to protect us from the things that we feel may hurt us-and failure is no different. The one thing to remember though, is that fear is not real. Fear exists because our mind displays this in an effort to stop us from getting hurt. We often allow this protection method to stop us from doing the things we don't feel comfortable doing.

Let's take sales people for example. It might be a fear of making phone calls to strangers, or speaking in front of a group that causes them to not take action. For others, it could be the fear of being rejected for a position that they don't feel they are fully skilled for, or any other opportunity that has them second guessing it.

Either way, allowing ourselves to fall into the rut of making excuses will prohibit us from making any positive changes forward towards a better life. It will help to recognize that excuses are a symptom of bad thinking and that we should get over them fast.

THREE: The *force of average* makes procrastination and flat out laziness a priority

Have you ever taken something that was supposed to be done in a day and pushed it off to the next day? Sure you have! I have done this and probably everybody else on the planet has. It's easy to let procrastination seep in because it feels so good in the moment to put it off. We had a task that should have been done today, but we can do that tomorrow.

Sound familiar?

Procrastination is the delayer of dreams and delays us in achieving our goals. It takes less effort to just push what we were supposed to do today off to the next day-which by the way, never gets done.

Sure there will be times where you may have to switch some item from one day to the next. But if you allow this to happen on a regular basis, you will lower your productivity through your reluctance, and that's when you really get nowhere-fast.

FOUR: The *force of average* will keep you in your current situation and state of mind

Have you ever wondered why successful people stand out in the market more than others? Take for example that guy at your work you don't like who keeps getting a raise or your friend who bought a new car while you're still driving your beater.

Truth be told, successful people do the little things that add up to a successful path. Often people don't see all the little things that successful people have done-leading them to the bigger wins. Successful people want more out of life and they go after it. The people that allow themselves to stay in their current situation allow the *force of average* to keep them there.

Have you ever heard someone talk about a person who is successful as if they are just lucky to be that way? Maybe you are guilty of doing this too? Society looks at rich people in this way, making the assumption they were born with a silver spoon. I know some were. However, most weren't. While many people are born rich, most are self made, through their own efforts. If you're only thinking average and not willing to change your state of mind, you will be stuck in an average life, wishing things were different.

FIVE: The *force of average* wants you to accept average and think that you can't do the great things you want to

Many people accept average and live a life that they are content with. While I don't feel there is anything wrong with someone being content in their life, I do feel that people have no right to complain if they are not where they want to be. The *force of average* is a powerful force that is around us in the world. The *force of average* doesn't want you to think you are above average and capable of being great. This force will use anything at its disposal to keep you from creating an above average life for yourself.

Did you get bad grades in school?

You won't be successful.

Do you have a disability?

You won't be successful.

Do you feel you are not worthy?

You won't be successful.

These are some of the things that could run through your mind in an effort to keep you accepting average. If we don't allow ourselves to think we can do bigger and better things in life, we remain under the *force of average*.

To really understand why you are not happy with your current life, we need to dive deeper and ask ourselves these questions.

Am I really living a life that I love?

While not every day will be filled with roses, you should generally enjoy what you do. If you don't have an ambition for your work or if you wake up uninspired every morning, this is a sign that you don't enjoy what you do. Take a moment to jot down the pros and cons of what you are currently doing to figure out if a change is needed in this area.

Do I dread going in on Monday, or going to work in general?

We all know someone who complains about the weekend being too short, or they praise God that it's Friday. We even hear people talking about Wednesday as hump day because it's the middle of the week and they made it! What a terrible way to live. You should be driven most days and be happy about your day. If you're not happy with what you're doing daily, then you won't perform the activities that will lead to success. You will stay down for the count.

Do I feel worthless at my current job?

There are some situations where an employer will make you feel worthless at your job, or a customer or client berates you at your business. This does not mean you need to accept the situation. Humans are not trees stuck in one place, but smart creatures that can change our future, should we choose to. On this same note, you can feel like your current opportunity is not challenging you enough or utilizing your skill set. These should be indicators that it's time for a change.

Will I have advanced in my opportunity in 3, 5, or even 10 years?

It's important to really look at current opportunity to see if you will have a chance to advance further down the road. There's no point in putting in a bunch of effort for a dead end job with no future opportunities. Look at your career or business 3, 5 and even 10 years down the road to see if it makes sense for you to stay.

Am I fed up with where I'm at in life professionally and personally?

Are you happy where you're at professionally? Personally? If you said no to one or both of these questions, then it's time for a change. It's a terrible feeling to be fed up with a situation that you're in, or settling for something that you don't love. Also, if you're not happy in your professional life, that could affect your personal life as well, or vice versa. Whether it's the professional or personal life that needs changing, recognize that it needs to be done.

When you ask yourself these questions, it brings you to a point of self realization that maybe you do want more out of life. That maybe you shouldn't be settling for average because you are not feeling fulfilled by what you currently do. How can you be excited about your life if you don't have passion for your endeavors? Hopefully these questions will be a real eye opener for you and bring you to the realization that a change needs to happen in your life.

What defines an average life?

In order to figure out what an average life looks like, we must look at what defines it. All of us will have a slightly different definition of what they feel an average life is, so I have come up with the top six definitions that I feel are the most pertinent.

ONE: People work without really getting ahead

It's safe to say that many people will work pretty hard at their job because it feels like the right thing to do. They will show up and put in just enough effort to not get fired. The problem lies in that they don't look at getting ahead in what they're doing. Sure they might complain about opportunities sliding past them in some attempt to keep them where there at, but if they aren't looking for opportunity, how would they know it if they even saw it?

Average people work hard and fail to recognize opportunity that is presented to them, only to blame others for their bad luck. They also don't create opportunity for themselves as they go through life stuck in the same spot without much of anything.

TWO: They barely survive Monday through Friday

How many people do you know who complain about the work week, their boss or their duties? I know countless people who fall into this category. Average people complain about how their boss is doing them wrong, or their job is not fair. They rant about how Suzy in HR got the promotion when it should have been their's. They hover around the break room talking drama and sharing useless gossip about other people. They go on social media platforms and share how bad their day is going and how life isn't fair. You see average people run rampant in society too!

There is no limit to the amount of complaints and excuses that are shared by average people who just get by and survive the work week, or whatever wo¯k schedule they have, as if it's a plague or pandemic that was thrust upon them.

THREE: They complain about how hard life is and how bad things are for them

I'm sure you have heard the phrase misery loves company. This couldn't be truer of average people. Average people complain daily telling others how hard their life is and how all these bad things happen to them all the time. They go on to share how life seems to have it out for them because they can never have a good day. While bad things can happen to any one of us, it seems to be a constant in an average person's life and routine. It's almost as if they seek out the drama and terrible events in an effort to feel normal. The worst part about it is that average people don't want solutions to their problems; they just want to share the negativity with others to feel better for the moment.

Think about it.

You come across someone who is absolutely miserable about their job or circumstances, you or someone else offers a possible solution, and they don't act on it. You tell your colleague or co-worker that maybe they should get a new job elsewhere, and you're met with a "why should I do that" look on their face.

If someone knows how to fix a problem they're having, and they don't, that's pure laziness. People who are above average will welcome any solutions that may improve their life for the better. Above average people are always wanting to learn more and do more with their life.

The problem with this type of behavior I just mentioned is that it won't get you out of living an average life. By consistently thinking and sharing negative thoughts with yourself and others, you won't allow the positive thoughts and solutions to come in.

FOUR: They live for the weekends and vacations

People who choose to live an average life tend to live for the weekends like they wi.l find the Holy Grail once Friday approaches. You probably know a handful of people who act this way. Maybe at this moment you are one of them. Average people can't get half way through the week without sharing how hard their week is going so far. These people can't wait for the weekend to come around. They even thank the lord when Friday has arrived.

You don't have to look far to find this type of thinking either. As you scroll through social media you see someone who posts their vacation pictures while telling people how they don't want to leave the destination and go back to their regular average life. They may eve say something like "I wish my vacation was longer!" While there is nothing wrong with looking forward to the weekend or a vacation, if you dread the rest of your days and your routine you are returning to, then you have fallen victim to the *force of average*.

FIVE: They wish they were young again

I don't think you will ever hear a person who is living their dream life talk about wishing they were younger solely because they would do things differently. Don't get me wrong here, part of me wishes I was in my twenties again! But when you know someone who enjoys their life and what they do, it's because they value the experience they gained and enjoy the life there currently living. People who have beat the *force of average* look forward to moving forward and progressing through life with motivation and love.

Average people often dwell on their younger years of happiness and youthfulness. Just the thought of their future years possibly being the best ever never really crosses their mind. They refer to their youth as the glory days-implying that their present days are not glorious or thrilling.

SIX: They dream of retirement

There are a lot of people who have spent decades in a career doing work that they enjoyed and when their retirement years begin to approach, they get more and more excited about retiring. While this is certainly the right feeling to have, we won't be talking about those people in this section.

I'm referring to the people who live unhappily through decades of unsatisfying work fantasizing about how good retirement will be and how happiness will surround them once they get out of their horrible job. These people look at retirement as a moment where they can do whatever they want, whenever they want, and everything will finally be perfect. Their life will finally be complete.

The problem with this thinking is that it provides a false sense of pleasure, because tomorrow is not guaranteed. You can wake up and go through your morning routine, go out into the world, and never return home. If you live an average life and the promise of tomorrow never comes, you will have wasted a whole life to mediocrity.

It's ok to have a big goal and something to look forward to in the coming years. But if you don't enjoy what you are currently doing to reach that goal, or make any changes to live a life you truly want to live, then chances are you won't be much happier should you reach retirement. Even worse, you will be dreading the process of getting to retirement.

Do any of these six things just describe you?

Do you know at least three people who do any or all of these things?

Chances are you do. It's important to understand that while some people will enjoy a life like this, many don't. It's fine to live an average life, provided you don't complain about it. I don't feel that anyone living this type of life has any right to complain because they are not choosing to make the changes to improve their life and overcome the *force of average*.

There are people every day who live this type of life and they are content with how things are going. I have to admit I admire that. Chances are those people would not be reading a book on the topic of not being average. This book is for those who are looking for tips and strategies to create a life they truly want to live and do the type of work they really want to do. Because as many have said, Life is too short to be doing something you don't want to do. And since you have a choice, why settle for an average life anyway?

Why do so many people settle for average?

Why is it some people can beat the *force of average* while others struggle? Are they just born lucky, or is there something they did to achieve the level of success they were seeking? Why do some people find success and others struggle financially or emotionally or both?

We know there are things in life that are destined to be. We know that trees can't move from where they are planted. We know that animals are born every day with the intention to do what animals before them have done repeating the cycle over and over again.

Humans, on the other hand, are not meant to repeat what their parents have done before them, and their parents before them, unless it's something they enjoy doing. When I think of my own kids and what I want for them, I think of them having the resources to pursue what they feel is a truly successful life, one that they created for themselves. Not a life that I pushed them to go into.

So why do most people live an average life and never reach their full potential? Is it an issue where each generation does about average; not having the motivation to break free from the cycle? How do some people beat the *force of average* and excel in their life?

Unlike many other species, humans have a choice to grow to

live a life they designed for themselves. A life where they don't thank God it's Friday and call Wednesday 'hump day' while going through the motions. Humans can create a positive change in their life and pursue what motivates them to wake up every day and hit the ground running. And you don't have to settle for less either!

Chances are you are reading this in an effort to beat the *force of average* that was forced upon you by society and even your peers. The great news is you can do greater things in life if you apply what I share in this book to your daily routine, efforts and life.

Here are four reasons why I think people stay stuck in 'average mode':

ONE: They don't feel that they are worthy of success

Average people don't have a belief system in place to allow them to feel that they are worthy of achieving success. They go through life thinking they are not worthy of winning, therefore failing before they even begin.

TWO: They are content with an average life-yet still complain about it

I understand perfectly that not everybody is looking to be a rock star in their life and that not everyone wants to change their life, or reach for those big opportunities. Many people are content in where they are at in their life, career and relationship. As a matter of fact, to me that is the definition of success. Where I feel these people make the mistake is that they sometimes still complain about their situation without restraint to anyone with an open ear. The reality is that it takes less effort to frown than it does to smile.

THREE: They associate defeat with failure

I feel this is the biggest hurdle for so many people. Many associate defeat with failure, because they didn't win what they were going after. They don't start the business they wanted, or apply for that job opportunity they came across, because they visualized failing at it before they even went after it. Successful people don't view failure as defeat. They view failure as a learning opportunity with a chance to come up with another solution or tailor what they were offering. Successful people know that you don't fail at something, you simply learn from it. By the way, most successful people fail far more than they win.

FOUR: They don't know what they really want

Average people tend to have no real direction, or no clear path, for their lives, because they have no idea what makes them tick, what motivates them, or what they are passionate about. They wander aimlessly throughout each day wanting to get the day over with. How can you go after something you want if you don't know what that is? Truth be told, average people don't really go after much in their life. They don't sit down with themselves and jot down the very things they want, or would like, out of life. Sure, they will tell you they want a better life, or that they want this or that, but they have no specific idea of what that entails.

To get to where you want to go, you have to know what that looks like for you. You have to be specific about your needs and aspirations so that you can be guided towards the right direction.

Successful people know what they want, what they are passionate about, and they create a plan to go after it with daily effort. They have done the homework to figure out what gets them motivated and moving passionately. By making these simple changes in your life, you can look forward to living your life how you want to, on your own terms. You will have the clarity of knowing exactly what you want, which will lead to you be driven to go after it with a much clearer vision.

I just shared with you four reasons why people stay stuck in their lives, accepting the *force of average*. While these reasons are based on my opinion, I would say they accurately describe why many people stay stuck in place - in an average state.

Further into this book, you will read about my personal story of how I changed my own life for the better, as well as some other success stories on how everyday people took charge of their lives and created a life they look forward to. We will dive into tips on overcoming challenges such as self doubt, changing your mindset, becoming more decisive and various other tips. I will share how you can take that first step out of your comfort zone to change your mindset so that you can see things differently and take advantage of opportunity that comes your way.

After reading this book, you will be armed with the real world advice that you can apply to transform your life - provided you want to make the change. Use the tips in this book to beat the *force of average* for yourself so that you can reach your full potential. I warn you though; this book is only for those looking to conquer the *force of average*, and not for those who are currently happy where they are at.

I am living proof that when you make positive changes in your life, you can open up a world of opportunity for yourself. Before I became successful, I was a wandering wreck. I hated the jobs I held, dreading Mondays and looking forward to the weekend, or a break. Not to mention my money wasn't good. The good news is I didn't stay stuck in that rut. When I realized that I was capable of so much more, I pushed through and beat the *force of average*, and I did it with the tips I share in this book. The turning point for me was when I had reached a point where I couldn't imagine doing what I was doing for the rest of my life, and that a change was needed.

One of the reasons why I wrote this book is to inspire others to overcome whatever challenges they are facing and to share how they can change the direction of their life, so that they wake up every day exhilarated and filled with purpose. I couldn't imagine going back to the life where I wasn't excited about what I was doing. I wouldn't dream of being stuck in a dead end job without any opportunity to advance, or to be a part of something great. I know what it feels like to be in a position where I hated going to a job that did little to motivate me, other than provide me a basic check; which wasn't enough to live on! I have been in those jobs where I was counting down the time until it was quitting time.

Talk about a dull life!

The good news is you don't have to live life that way. You don't have to be stuck hoping that you will find something better, or that your luck will change. You will be a person of action and you make things happen in your life. You will create good luck for yourself, the kind that you thought only others could have.

When you commit to making the decision to make a positive change in your life, you will be on your way to beating the *force of average*. You can take control over your life and start going down a path where great things can happen for you. You will start seeing the little differences that will lead you to the big differences in your life.

Make no mistake. This is not some jump up and down while doing cart wheels approach to a better life. This is a real decision that you, and only you, can make to really change your trajectory and benefit from doing so.

Think about this for a moment.

Would you want the pain of regret when you are older and in your autumn years?

Would you want to feel that you didn't really do everything you could in this life to be your best?

When you decide that the time to change your life is now, then you will start to see things differently. You will focus on putting yourself in front of opportunities that put you in a better position.

Will it be hard? Of course it will! I never said this would be easy.

You know what else is hard? Living an average life.

I've learned that anything worth having is always going to be a challenge. But guess what? It won't be impossible! I also learned that the road to success is a windy and treacherous road, filled with bumps and obstacles. You will be able to apply what you've learned from this book to navigate you down the bumpy path to success. Does it sound scary? It's really not. I would rather have a hard day, week, or year working on my career than be working in a dead end job with no opportunity for the rest of my life. I would rather conquer the treacherous road towards success, because it will provide much more than the road to average.

Today is the day you could draw the line in the sand and demand more for yourself. To make the choice to learn what you need to know so that you can fight back and break free from the *force of average.* Today is the day you could learn how to be a powerful force in your own life-and to eliminate average from your lifestyle.

Loving what you do

It's extremely important to love what you do day in and day out. This is a major reason why many people find success to begin with, because they found something that they love doing and they don't mind putting in the effort necessary to really stand out. When you have a passion for your work, you won't experience burn out because you will have a deep rooted passion for what you're doing. The work won't feel like work. This doesn't mean you have to work 80 hours a week and not have work-life balance. It helps to love what you do to be happy in your life and overcome the challenges that will present itself.

Does having a passion for what you do sound like another cliché statement by some self proclaimed life coach? Maybe. The question to ask yourself is, "Could I be happy in a career or job that I don't love most of the time?" Chances are you said no. There is one differentiator between those that succeed and those who don't, they love what they do. They do their work mostly with a smile on their face.

There's a reason why some people excel at their career while others don't. Successful people, or people who are happy in their work, have an internal desire that drives them to complete the work they do. They live, breathe and consume it. Having a passion for what you do get's you through those rough days that come about. When you love what you do, you don't look at the clock and countdown to quitting time. You don't thank God it's Friday or despise the rise of Monday morning. When you have a passion for your work, you will wake up invigorated and ready to conquer your goal(s).

Does this mean you will love your career or business every day no matter what? Of course not! But with passion, it will be easier to get through the challenges that present themselves because you will have the bigger picture in mind. When you love what you do, you will think bigger, work harder, and achieve so much more. I make it my mission to live everyday with purpose and drive, because I don't dread my work or life. This is something I created for myself, and I know you can do the same for yourself.

I will be sharing with you the very steps I implemented to get out of a life without purpose and passion. There is nothing more gratifying then waking up with a feeling of purpose that you are doing something great in your life. You will look forward to whatever it is you will be doing, whether it's a project, or a goal you are working towards.

Have you ever been driving during what is called the 'rush hour'? If you're not familiar with this term, it's the period in the morning and right before dinner where a mass amount of people are rushing to get to work. The next time you are in traffic during these time frames, take a glance at some of the people driving.

Are they smiling?

Do they appear happy?

Are they tuned out to everyone around them?

Or are they exhibiting sadness, dullness or anxiety? This may be a little judgmental, but I would bet it's true for most. And considering that many people are not happy with their work, I would say the majority are dreading going to work.

Unfortunately, not many people realize this important lesson in life; ever. The good news is that it doesn't have to be this way. You don't have to accept what the *force of average* does to you. You have the ability to create a life that you actually look forward to and want to wake up to; a life where you don't dream of the weekend as a getaway from your awful week.

Does this sound easier than it is?

Yes. I'm not going to lie, it takes work.

It takes a change in your mindset. It takes creating new habits while breaking old ones. It takes reading this book and applying these tips to your life. If you make the choice to make a positive change while moving forward toward your new life, I promise you it will be well worth it.

I am living proof!

I had the extreme pleasure of being interviewed by Pire Jones Grossman with Authority Magazine about how I began my second chapter in my own life and how I beat the *force of average* myself. This was an important interview that I feel you could benefit from reading. The term Second Chapter describes how I made a major change in my own life to live life on my own terms, while earning the success I sought.

Here is the interview:

Pire Jones Grossman: Can you tell us a bit about your childhood back story?

I was your typical young boy who grew up in Southeast Michigan just North of Detroit. I had a passion for video games, comedy movies and hanging out with friends every chance I got. I also loved to read. I remember reading every single Hardy Boys book available in the middle school's library. I always found books fascinating. But life wasn't always pleasant for me. Throughout middle school I developed major behavioral issues and could not keep my impulses at bay. I would disrupt classes and even get suspended. This behavior led me to have to repeat the 6th grade. That was a terrifying moment that scarred me for years to come. Eventually, I straightened up and graduated high school. But I had to take one summer school class after graduation, but they let me walk the stage. Looking back, I realized that these experiences would be the building blocks leading me to where I am today.

Can you please give us your favorite "Life Lesson Quote"? Can

you share how that was relevant to you in your life?

One of the life quotes that I live by is a quote from Zig Ziglar. "You can get everything in life you want if you will just help enough other people get what they want." This reminds me of my mission to help others in my own efforts. To help as many people as possible.

How would your best friend describe you?

It's funny because I actually asked my good friend this question not too long ago. My best friend said he would describe me as a man on a mission. A person who puts value forth for others to benefit from. A guy who is driven and goes after his goals with ambition and a hard work ethic.

You have been blessed with much success. In your opinion, what are the top three qualities that you possess that have helped you accomplish so much?

I have been blessed with more success than I would have ever thought. While sometimes I do feel 'lucky', I would say that my good luck has come from these three things. The first is self confidence. Having the self confidence to go out and do what I do to achieve success is key. The second is having a very strong work ethic. After all, a person with less talent can go out and outwork somebody who simply works less. I have always worked hard at all my jobs, but when I applied a strong work ethic to my second chapter, that's when I really took off.

The third is to surround myself with supporters of my cause. For me this one is about family. I'm not a huge time management focused guy. I feel life will push us out of whack at times. Having a strong family that supports me in my efforts has really played a large part in my success. I simply would not be where I am at today if it weren't for my family and support system.

Let's now shift to the main part of our discussion about 'Second Chapters'. Can you tell our readers about your career experience before your Second Chapter?

I really did not have much of a career, or really much of anything to look forward to professionally prior to reinventing myself and finding success in my current profession. I held a series of hourly jobs that I hated while counting down the hours before clocking out. I had no real goals, or ambition to make more money, or to be a success. I went through the motions and collected a paycheck. I hated my jobs and was never really excited to work for the supervisors that I had. I was coasting through life like a ship without a sail.

And how did you "reinvent yourself" in your Second Chapter?

One of the defining moments of my life where I really considered reinventing myself was when I was introduced to the mortgage industry through a family member. I met my wife some years earlier and was really inspired by her commitment to her goals and achievements. Her big goal was to have employment in the healthcare field as an RN. I watched her study for tests and together we would spend hours in the libraries. That was when I decided that enough is enough. It was time to pursue my own goals and to design a life that best suited me. I decided to take the plunge to become a professional sales person. Something inside of me didn't want to be where I was. I certainly did not want to continue making the lower income that I was making in those jobs. That was the point in my life where I became fed up with my situation and decided to change direction and reinvent myself. Once I made that decision I never looked back.

Can you tell us about the specific trigger that made you decide that you were going to "take the plunge" and make your huge transition?

The specific trigger that made me take the plunge into my second chapter was when my wife and I were talking about marriage and our future life together. I was also inspired by her tenacity towards achieving her goal of a Bachelors Degree in Nursing. I came to the realization that I really did not want to be doing the back breaking physical labor that I was doing for the rest of my life. This was the pivotal point where I took the plunge and decided that my future would be a better one! One that I truly designed for myself. For such a long time I was being reactive in my jobs and in life. I was hoping that somebody else would design my life for me. It was time for me to take action and make things happen.

What did you do to discover that you had a new skill set inside of you that you haven't been maximizing? How did you find that and how did you ultimately overcome the barriers to help manifest those powers?

I've been often told that I have a personality perfect for sales, but I never really knew how to hone in on that skill. Going back to my childhood, I was that kid who could not sit still. I would get bored easily and get into trouble often. Growing into becoming a young man, I was really not inspired by boring jobs and mundane tasks. Taking the plunge into a sales position such as the mortgage industry really seemed to fit me well.

One of the major challenges I had to overcome was a speech impediment. Going through my childhood with a speech impediment was not easy. I was very outgoing, but I would experience multiple occasions when I would stutter or stammer. Defending myself oftentimes led to fights and suspensions from school. I had to work hard at trying to sound somewhat normal when I spoke. Fast forward to the point in my life where I wanted to reinvent myself, I had to work hard at not only getting over the self doubt that I had but I also had to make my speech sound fluent and normal.

One of the best ways I overcame those barriers was to dive in and gain as much information about what I was selling so that I could be more confident in my communication. Mastering this habit became a real confidence booster, because I knew what I needed to say and how to say it. I would also read as much as I could about presenting and selling. While I did not improve overnight, I saw myself actually getting better at speaking and communicating with clients. This really gave me the confidence to think bigger and to actually set goals of being better at my craft. This was the first step towards success in my second chapter.

How are things going with this new initiative?

I am at a place in my life where I never thought I would be. The level of success keeps rising for me, due to the implementation of the skills that I have learned. If you would have asked the younger version of me if I would experience the level of success I am experiencing at this point, I would have thought you were crazy. Yet here I am. While I am enjoying every day of this journey, I am not looking to stay at this level. Every day I am driven to pursue more out of life. To be more, and be a better version of myself than I was before.

Many people gain some success and then hang out at that level. For me the success that I have had is fuel for my fire. It shows me that I can up my game and succeed at an even higher level. To increase the size of my goals and to gain new skills. If you were to look at my written goals today verses years ago, you would see a massive difference. When you reinvent yourself, you learn that you can be so much more in life than you think. It really gives you the drive and energy to go after bigger goals and make bigger plans.

Is there a particular person who you are grateful towards who helped get you to where you are? Can you share a story about that?

One of the biggest drivers in my success has been my wife Erica. Whether she knew it or not, she was inspiring me in the early days to really want more out of life. When my wife and I met I was a laborer without a plan. I had no real goals and no real future. Seeing her work at her goal of obtaining a Bachelors Degree in Nursing really made me think about my own future. I came from a good childhood with great parents that loved me and provided the things that we needed to have a nice life, but I was still struggling with my speech impediment and my hyper active behavior. It wasn't until I met my wife that I really started to direct that focus into something positive and into an endeavor that has now created a much better life than I would have ever imagined.

Can you share the most interesting story that happened to you since you started in this new direction?

After years of having success in the mortgage industry, I decided to make the move to become a REALTOR. I had enjoyed my time in the mortgage sector, but was looking for a more enjoyable profession. Not a career that had me locked inside an office all day. One of the first defining moments and most interesting story from my second chapter was when I won my first award for my role as a REALTOR. I was with a broker for a short time and won the prestigious Rookie of the Year Award. My wife and I got dressed up and attended the broker's annual awards show. This was a fancy event where all the agents in the office met to mingle as well as possibly take home an award. I will never forget that night as my wife and I were seated at our table with some of my colleagues. They had been giving out awards for a little while when it happened. They announced my name!

As I look back at the picture my wife snapped of me standing up and heading to the podium, I can still remember the tingle that went through me. That huge feeling of accomplishment as the room applauded for me. It was the most interesting and monumental time I can remember. This was proof that I had found my niche. My second chapter had seen some success. My peers, family and friends saw that I had changed and that I had embarked on a journey that would change my life forever.

Did you ever struggle with believing in yourself? If so, how did you overcome that limiting belief about yourself? Can you share a story or example?

This is a hard question. I really struggled with believing in myself and that I was capable of doing great things. Thinking that I would be successful was never really a consideration until I decided to start my second chapter. This was accelerated when I was exposed to what my wife was striving for in college. Without that experience I probably would have ended up just coasting through life maintaining a job that I hated and not experiencing the level of success that I have currently. Overcoming this challenge became easier as I decided that I was going to reinvent myself and to create a better life by learning what I needed to be successful. I am a firm believer that all of the answers we need are in books. I started reading books about my profession and teaching myself everything that would make me better and sharpened. Knowledge may be power, but knowledge with implementation is the real power. Knowing what you need to know and then implementing what you have learned is what really makes someone successful.

In my own work I usually encourage my clients to ask for support before they embark on something new. How did you create your support system before you moved to your new chapter?

For me one of my biggest supporters was my wife. But I also had the support of those around me. My parents and my in-laws were very supportive and encouraged me to pursue my second chapter. Having a strong support system helps. It keeps you moving forward on days where you just don't feel it. Seeking out people who I know are supportive was key in my success.

Starting a new chapter usually means getting out of your comfort zone, how did you do that? Can you share a story or example of that?

I will never forget when I first started in the mortgage industry. There was no training or help offered at all. I was pointed to an empty office and given a phone book to make phone calls in an attempt to refinance the mortgages of strangers. Not only was I very nervous about this job, I was also stammering over the phone like you would not believe. The fact that I was outgoing helped a little, but not much. I remember how I would be sweating heavily as I would dial the phone thinking of how I might mess up what I was going to say. I showed up to that office daily determined to conquer the fear. I would not allow that fear to hold me back from success and where I wanted to be. I reminded myself that if this profession did not work that I would be back where I was. I surely did not want that to happen. I had to step out of my comfort zone and tackle the task.

- End of interview-

As you just read, my life was not always easy. My past has taught me how to appreciate what I have so much more, because I had to work for it; and I continue to do so. I learned that you can never own success; it can only be rented through your daily actions and habits. You must always be a student of learning to accomplish what you want out of life.

Here are twenty-five tips that I've learned to beat the *force of average* and create a life I look forward to. I credit my success to these valuable tips. I know they can work for you too.

ONE: Realize a Change Is Needed In Your Life

TWO: Change Your Mindset, Change Your Life

THREE: Limiting Beliefs Are Just That-Limiting

FOUR: Discovering Your 'Why'

FIVE: Self-Doubt Sucks, Overcome It!

SIX: Recognizing Fear, And Conquering It

SEVEN: Believing You Are Worthy

EIGHT: Birds Of a Feather Flock Together

NINE: Age Is Just a Number

TWENTY-FOUR: It's Your Life, So Start Living It!

TWENTY-FIVE: Successful People Share Their Stories

I just shared with you the sections we will cover in this book. Each part is a valuable tip that, if learned and implemented, will allow you to beat the *force of average* in your life. Now that you have a better idea of what will be covered, it's time to dive into the lessons.

"Change is painful, but nothing is as painful as staying stuck somewhere you don't belong"

- *Mandy Hale*

REALIZE A CHANGE
IS NEEDED

In order to make a positive change in your life you need to recognize that a change is actually needed. If you decide that you are happy with how your life is at the moment, then this book is not for you.

After all, it's ok to be satisfied with how things are going for yourself. But if you have come to the realization that you are in fact not satisfied with where you are, or where you are headed, then it's time to make the change.

Everyone's perception of a happy life will be different, so you must look at your inner self to come up with the things that you feel would make your life better or more rewarding. Think deeply about the things that will have you waking up feeling ecstatic and ready for the day. At first, this may seem daunting or frustrating when you think about brainstorming what would make a happier life for yourself, but I assure you it's not as hard as you think.

To help you get started, I have put together a list of questions to ask yourself:

Would I be happier if I had a different job?

What really makes me happy or excited about waking up?

Do I feel as though my current job is fulfilling?

Am I heading down a path that I will want to be on when I'm older?

Am I doing everything I can to find opportunity in my life?

Do I dread Monday's and thank God it's Friday?

Do I complain a lot about my daily routine?

Would I be better off in a different environment?

Do I have a good circle of friends that motivate and encourage me?

What am I passionate about? And am I doing these things?

Would those around me say I am happy with my life?

Perhaps it's the material things you crave.

Would I be happier if I had a new car, boat or house?

Do I wish I had a bigger or better home?

Do I like the clothes I wear?

Do I need to buy that expensive item?

After your brainstorming session, you should have a general idea of whether or not a real change is needed in your life. By asking yourself these questions and jotting down your answers, you will realize that a problem exists allowing you to come up with the solution(s) for your life. When I was looking to make a change in my own life, I was looking into different career paths and what each of those offered in terms of opportunities. I had my own brainstorming session about what I liked and didn't like about work and other deciding factors, such as pay and schedule. Jotting down what was in my head at the time really helped clarify the problem I had while allowing me to move forward towards a better life.

It's a huge benefit to write all the ideas you have onto paper without reservation, so you can better understand yourself and your motivations. This process will give you an idea of where you're at and where you would like to be, or what you would like to achieve in your life. Without figuring this part out, it will be that much harder to get to where you want to be.

"You've got to win
in your mind
before you win
in your life"

- John Addison

CHANGE YOUR MINDSET CHANGE YOUR LIFE

TWO

Experts say the human brain is one of the most powerful wonders of the world. Unlike any other species, humans are able to change the course of their life any way they see fit. A dog is destined to be a dog. A tree is meant to only grow in its current spot. But a human can make any change they see fit to better their life. If you don't like something in any part of your life, you can implement change to make it better. You are capable of creating so much more for yourself, and those around you.

A major part in recognizing this capability is your mindset, and the role it plays. Your mindset is a large part of whether or not you are happy or sad, content or discontent, successful or not. Your mindset can play a huge factor in whether or not you do something.

When you decide to change your mindset, you are choosing to think more differently than you have been. If you are looking to become someone different than who you are currently, or change where you are at, then you need to change your mindset to reflect who you want to become. Learning and knowing how to stay in the right mindset can mean a world of difference, while keeping you on track towards your goals. If you choose the wrong mindset, it will do the exact opposite - keeping you where you are currently at. We know this when something terrible happens to us during the day. The wrong mindset would tell you that you had a terrible day. The right mindset would tell you that you had a bad five minutes or so. Maintaining a positive mindset will make it easier for you to deal with the hurdles you face in life. The right mindset will also keep you on track towards your new life, and you will resolve negative issues much faster.

This is a lesson I wish I learned earlier in my life. It wasn't until my adult years that I figured out how to change my mind set to reflect the person I wanted to become. I didn't have the right mindset and wasn't focusing on the choices that would get me closer to what I wanted out of life. Changing my mindset meant I had to envision the person I wanted to become, and act in such a way that I would be perceived as that person. I wanted to become much more than what I was at that moment in my life, and learning about the power of my mindset accelerated my efforts into making that happen. It was this lesson and focus that led me to be the successful professional I am today, someone who provides value to others daily. I envisioned myself as this person; which kept my vision top of mind and keeping my mindset right.

This is not to say that you should fake it until you make it.

That's horrible advice. It's important to be authentic, with a clear vision of who you want to be while you pursue becoming that person. See yourself as the person you want to be and present yourself in that manner. From my very first day as a salesperson, I projected myself as a professional seeking to help others solve their problems. Even when I was just starting out, I walked, talked, and acted the part and I remained authentic in my actions.

When you have a positive mindset, it will be contagious to others. You will have the power to motivate others to be more receptive to what you have to offer. People like to communicate and do business with people that they like. The same goes for employers looking to hire new employees.

You may be asking how we go about changing our mindset for the better.

Here are six effective ways you can change your mindset:

ONE: Accept that your thinking needs changing

Once you learn that you need to change your mindset for the better, you can make the necessary adjustments towards the right thinking. Once these adjustments are made, it will allow more openness to the success you desire. You should never allow a negative mindset to rob you of your goals and ambitions, or to distract you from what you need to do daily. Keeping that positive mindset will help get you through whatever life throws your way, without the higher level of stress that could occur. Does this mean that every day will be filled with roses and happiness? No! You need to accept that your thinking has to stay on the right path to achieve what you want. Remember, the right mindset will keep you productive and working towards your goal(s) without fail.

TWO: Stay focused on your long term vision

Focusing on your long term vision will help keep your mindset in the right place. When you know what you want to achieve long term, it's easier to stay focused and stay the course. You can do this by simply keeping a picture of your long term goal(s) in front of you, to inspire you to implement the daily actions you must take to be successful. Many times people stay stuck in an average life because they don't have a long term vision of how they want their life to be. They think short term all too often. On your quest towards your new life, think of where you want to be long term. You can even go a step further and think about where you want to be in 3, 5 or even 10 years from now. Be sure to write these down in a journal also.

THREE: Start by gaining small wins; celebrate them

Many times people set too big of a goal, only to feel like they've failed after working at it a short time. Gaining some small wins to get you closer to the bigger wins, you can celebrate the small successes that happen and use them as a stepping stone to keep your eye on the prize. An example of a small win could be that you finally registered for that online course to further your skills or you applied for a new job opportunity and were accepted. Smaller wins lead to b gger wins with the right mindset. You will have gained the courage you can use as fuel towards your bigger wins. Celebrate your small wins as they happen.

FOUR: Remind yourself of the positives

It's easy to get into a rut and forget about all the positive things that we have accomplished or the great things that exist in our life. We as humans tend to focus more on the negative things that happen to us instead of all the positive things that do. Reminding yourself of the positives in your life can not only change your mind set for the bette-, but it could turn a bad day into a good one.

Some ways to remind you of the positives in life could be reading something inspirational, looking through family pictures, reviewing the goals you set, to realign your mindset with your mission. This is why it's important to keep what you want in front of you and top of mind-which we talk about further in this book.

FIVE: Take in some reading

I believe that reading is the best way to keep our mind active and filled with great ideas. Taking in a good book should be a top priority and you should do it often. Whether you read fiction, or non-fiction, reading is a great exercise that can keep your mindset where it should be. I personally love to read topics about my industry to stay relevant. I also like to read about others who have achieved great things after going through hard times. Reading keeps my skill set strong and up to date. Choose whatever type of book you like to read and make that a part of your routine. Audio books are a great way to stay inspired. You can find just about anything on audio, which you can play in your car, or during your exercise routine. I make it a habit of having some form of inspirational audio in my car.

SIX: Review your goals

Reviewing your goals is a great way to keep you motivated, while keeping you on track towards what you want. If you fail to review the goals you set for yourself, it will be hard to stay on track and get anything done. Writing down your goals and keeping them in a place where they can be reviewed at a moment's notice is one of my keys to success. Reviewing your goals will keep you in the driver's seat as you head towards your new life. If you fail to review your daily goals, you will miss out on opportunity.

I invite you to implement these tips I just shared with you and figure out what you can do today to convert your mindset to one that benefits you personally and professionally. Once these tips become habits in your life, it will become easier to implement them.

"If you accept a limiting belief, then it will become a truth for you"

- *Louise Hay*

LIMITING BELIEFS ARE JUST THAT-LIMITING

One of the biggest obstacles people face that hinder the possibility of gaining success in any area are the limiting beliefs they say to themselves. Limiting beliefs are statements that limit your thinking in some way. These can be things you say to yourself when faced with a something new or a challenge that scares you.

Here are some examples of limiting beliefs:

ONE: "I can't..."

TWO: "I will never..."

THREE: "It's impossible to..."

FOUR: "There is no way I can..."

FIVE: "He or she is much better at..."

SIX: "They will never like how I..."

SEVEN: "People will think that..."

EIGHT: "I will fail if I..."

Limiting beliefs are caused by a number of factors which include the type of education you have, your childhood upbringing, or any negative experiences that have happened in your life. Maybe it's not you who has these limiting beliefs. Sometimes those around you will think they have the best intentions for you, and they may use some or all of these statements, thinking that they are protecting you from what you are about to do.

For example, someone who wants to start a business begins to share the idea with those around them, only to be told that most businesses fail and they shouldn't do that. Maybe someone is considering going back to school around their work schedule, only to be told that it will be too hard to juggle the class with current obligations. You must accept that these people don't know any better, and that you need to travel your own path towards the change you seek. No matter what you do, you will have people who project these limiting beliefs onto you.

If you allow these limiting beliefs to occupy your mind with full capacity, you will fail before you begin. Just saying these statements to yourself or others could train your mind and body to never take action towards what you really want out of life. It's important to turn these limiting beliefs into powerful, empowering beliefs that will have you taking action and bettering your situation.

When I learned this simple lesson, my view of the world changed, for the better. Empowering beliefs are a great way to remind yourself that you can do the impossible and go after what you want because you will believe you can.

Here are 20 examples of what empowering belief statements are:

ONE: "I believe in what I do"

TWO: "I am a confident person"

THREE: "I learn from my mistakes"

FOUR: "I can make a positive change in my life"

FIVE: "I am a strong person"

SIX: "I find meaning in my work"

SEVEN: "I am up for any challenge life throws at me"

EIGHT: "I love to learn new things"

NINE: "I am not afraid to ask for help"

TEN: "I am always open to new opportunity"

ELEVEN: "I love to try new things"

TWELVE: "I always value peoples feedback"

THIRTEEN: "Nothing is impossible to me"

FOURTEEN: "I can achieve my goals if I go after them"

FIFTEEN: "No task is too big for me"

SIXTEEN: "I am in charge of my own life"

SEVENTEEN: "I am not afraid of the future, only excited about the possibilities"

EIGHTEEN: "I hold myself accountable for my actions"

NINETEEN: "There are no failures, simply learning opportunities"

TWENTY: "My past does not define my future"

You just read some great examples of empowering beliefs that you can use in your own life to help eliminate those limiting beliefs. These are statements that you should write down and keep near you. Over time, your mind will be trained to think empowering thoughts without the negative limiting belief thoughts.

By the way, this is also great for setting your goals, which we talk about further in this book. Use the empowering beliefs I shared with you when writing out your goals so you can be aware of the possibilities of each goal.

For example: "I am a professional who strives to provide value to others while being the best in my industry".

"If we want to feel an undying passion for our work, if we want to feel we are contributing to something bigger than ourselves, we all need to know our 'WHY'."

- *Simon Sinek*

DISCOVERING YOUR 'WHY'

Just as a captain commands a ship, you must have a plan and know why you are setting out on your chosen journey to reach your destination effectively. It can be hard to charge your life if you don't know why you are doing it. Without direction, you would be wandering aimlessly without any idea of why you are about to do something.

Side note: *This is another reason why many people accept average in their life, because they don't know where they want to go.*

To put this into perspective, imagine a sail boat, without a sail, drifting aimlessly about the sea. Without a sail, the boat goes nowhere. This same rule applies to your life. Your reason why is your sail. Without knowing why you are about to do something, you won't be on a specific path; drifting aimlessly through your life.

One of the best lessons I've learned is having and knowing my 'why'. When you discover what your 'why' is and how powerful it is, you can gain the power to go out into the world with purpose and drive. This isn't just something that I came up with either. Many life coaches have shared the importance of knowing your 'why' with their students and followers. It's a very powerful method that we will dive into here.

The late Success Coach, Jim Rohn, shared this piece of advice, and it has revolutionized my life. Jim shared that to be successful, one of the things you absolutely need to know is your 'why'. You may be asking what exactly does this mean? Your 'why' is the absolute base of everything you do. You're 'why' is what get's you up and moving to do what you want to do daily. Your 'why' is what drives you to do the things you need to do whether it's a good day or bad.

Did you wake up tired and not feeling like going to work?

Remind yourself of your 'why' and get to it!

When you have a firm grasp on what your 'why' is, you can use it to break through the *force of average*. There won't be anything that will keep you down long when you have a strong 'why'. You will be an unstoppable force to be reckoned with.

Are you still trying to figure out what your 'why' is?

To fully understand the power of knowing your why, I have to share with you my 'why'. My 'why' is my family, my goals and all the things I want to achieve in my lifetime. My 'why' is what drives me to do the necessary daily routine and tasks to be the best that I can be in my life, personally and professionally. Your 'why' should be your motivator to get you on your feet and keep you moving forward.

Have you ever woken up tired and crabby? I know I have and sometimes still do. Reminding myself of my 'why' really motivates me to get back up to conquer the day. Just like reminding yourself of what your goals are, you need to remind yourself of why you are doing what you do. Your 'why' is your reminder that puts things back into perception and get's you back on your feet.

You may be asking yourself, is knowing my 'why' 100% guaranteed? In which my reply would be, no. Tomorrow is not guaranteed either. I can tell you that a person who uses their 'why' daily as their motivator will win far more, compared to someone who has no idea what their why is. It's just that powerful.

Knowing your 'why' can be an asset to you, because it can motivate you to take massive steps, to stay focused on your goals and to keep you moving towards your new life.

So what is your 'why'?

What really gets you going to achieve big things or at least get moving?

What get's your blood flowing in a positive way?

Still not sure what your 'why' is?

Here are three tips to help you define your 'WHY':

ONE: Identify the things that you can do to improve the lives of other people

Are there things you do, or strengths you have, that could improve the lives of others? Is there something you can offer that solves the problems that others may have? When you identify the things that you can do to help others, you will gain a level of self-confidence that is unmatched. When you know how you can benefit others, you will begin to go after opportunities without worry of failure or criticism. You will go out into the world with a sense of purpose and feel invigorated about your work or mission. Others will perceive you as a person of value that they can count on.

TWO: What makes you really feel alive?

If you could name something that really makes you come alive, what would that be? It could be a trip to an area you love, or a project that you think about often but never got around to. It could be that new car that you have seen around town that you wish you had. Perhaps it's a new home for you and your family. We all have things that really get us excited and moving. While they may be tied more to our personal side, it just might provide the insight you need to figure out where you want your life to head. Maybe you love to travel and could possibly look into a career that allows you to travel. Maybe it's something as simple as wanting to connect others to great resources, so you decide to be a networker.

You get the idea.

Grab a notepad and do a little brainstorming about what motivates you or makes you feel really good. Jot down all those things and then see if you can tie your work into these ideas. Then review what you have and consider the possibilities.

THREE: Where do you add the most value?

While we know it, or not, most of us have value that could really help someone else. You must figure out what your strengths are and identify what value you can offer, so that you can go out into the world with a passion. While passion alone is not enough to win at life, you must apply an unmatched work ethic to gain the success you desire. By adding value to the lives of others, you will be known as a trusted resource to them, and the success will follow.

I just shared with you three tips that you can apply to your life immediately to make a positive change in the right direction. I attribute a lot of my success to knowing what my 'why' is, and I know it will do the same for you.

Now that you have learned the power of knowing your 'why' and how it can get and keep you motivated, let's talk about what you should do next once you know what your 'why' is.

Write down all the things that comprise your 'why'. For me, I choose to keep my goals written down in a binder that I review daily. This method alone has really changed my life for the better. Take a moment to document all your goals with an image near each one, so that when you are not having a productive day or you are feeling sluggish, you can go to your goal binder and revive your sense of purpose.

Side tip: *Once you discover your 'why', keep it by your goals or where you can see it daily as a reminder for yourself. It could be the most important thing you read daily!*

"Doubt kills more dreams than failure ever will."

- Suzy Kassem

SELF-DOUBT SUCKS, OVERCOME IT!

FIVE

I'm a firm believer that self-doubt is the number one reason why people never reach their full potential. They don't think that they are good enough to be successful. They allow negative thoughts to run through their mind, stopping them dead in their tracks. They fail before they ever begin.

Self-doubt occurs when you allow your mind to convince yourself that you can't become something great, or that you don't have the resources to go after what you want out of life. Self-doubt will persuade you that you're not 'lucky enough' and that nobody will help you on your journey. If allowed, self doubt can spread like a cancer in your mind, never allowing you to overcome it.

From birth into our adulthood, we are taught by

others that we are average and that we shouldn't dream about big goals, or make big plans, because we probably won't achieve them. The influence around us may not actually call us average outright, but the influences and actions of others could influence your mind into thinking average.

We gaze at hugely successful people and think that they are lucky or gifted in what they do. But if you were to take a deeper look into the stories of many successful people, you would find that these people overcame challenges such as poverty, death of loved ones, diseases, or some life changing event and self-doubt. You would begin to realize that many successful people were not born lucky, coming from modest means, or even worse situations than you. You can use these positive life stories to help you overcome your own self-doubt when it strikes.

Why is it some people allow self-doubt to overrun their thoughts and keep them average in life?

Why do some allow self-doubt to keep them from believing they can be great in their own endeavors?

Is it because they have not had the little win's to provide them with the confidence to go after the bigger wins?

Is it because they don't feel they are worthy of great success?

Do they think they aren't good enough to be a high achiever?

Maybe someone close to them stated that they should be happy settling for what they have - average.

Did I just describe you?

When you look to beat the *force of average*, you must realize you can overcome self-doubt and begin to move forward towards the great things you seek, the very things that will make you happier and more successful in life. It's a powerful thing to know how to beat self-doubt so that you can move forward towards creating a better life.

When I was a youth I had a really bad speech impediment that felt like a curse throughout my grade school years. Every day I would go out into the world not looking forward to the interactions I would have with other kids. As I started a conversation, other kids would interrupt and finish my sentences while mocking how I sounded. I was plagued with people who thought a stutter was something to make fun of as they delivered their ridicule. You can imagine the self-doubt I had during this period of my life. It really had a hold on me.

As I look back at those years, I often think that my speech impediment held me back from doing the things I wanted to do, perhaps even hindering my enjoyment of those school years. Did I allow myself to succumb to the *force of average* by letting the opinion of others keep me down? At times I imagined myself failing before I ever got started, whether it was talking in groups or thinking of joining school clubs.

As I entered into my early 20's, I met a young woman who was going after her goal of becoming a Nurse. I tagged along and we spent hours together in libraries as she studied for her classes. I got to witness how she set goals for herself, which later led to her gaining a successful career. Watching her actions motivated me to make the decision to become more in life and to not settle for average. Her dedication and effort towards going after her goal(s) taught me that I could do the same, if I just replicate the effort.

While I still had much of my self-doubt lingering around, I became highly motivated by her drive and ambition to change the course of my own life. I wanted something of my own to go after. I didn't want to grow old in the dead end job that I held. I really wanted to overcome my self-doubt and pursue something that I could be proud of. I wanted to look forward to the work I was doing every day. After all, dreading each work day is no way to live.

Overcoming self-doubt is crucial to changing the direction of your life. When you realize that all your self-doubt is created from within, you can accomplish just about anything you want. When you crush that doubt and sell yourself on the idea that you can pursue your dreams, it's very empowering. And you can do it over and over again.

It's not enough for me to just tell you to overcome self-doubt. It's time to apply some actions to make it happen.

Here are eight tips to overcome your self-doubt:

ONE: Read about other successful people who overcame obstacles

Reading has the power to unlock doors to other worlds and information to help us mprove our lives for the better. Reading has empowered me to become better at my career. Anything you want to learn is at your fingertips through books, or on the internet. Pick some topics you are interested in and make it a priority to study them.

I have heard many people say that successful people are lucky to have what they have and that they were given success because they simply wanted it. As I mentioned earlier, when you really look deeper into the lives of successful people, you will find it's not that common they came from a really good background, or were handed everything they needed to become a success. The majority of people I have read about came from challenges that debilitated them for a time, things they had to overcome to get to where they are at today. The same goes for the hugely success people I have met in my life. Overcoming their self-doubt was one of those tips that led them to a better life.

There's nothing like being inspired by others who have gone through hell and back to become who they wanted to be in what they wanted to do. This should serve as a great reminder when you feel like you are having a bad day. Chances are somebody is having a much worse day than you and you should be grateful.

Reminding yourself of this fact can really put things into perspective.

TWO: Know that it is possible to achieve what you want

When I was younger, I didn't think that I could do great things. I had the mindset that I would end up somewhere working for the rest of my life in an average routine. It wasn't until my adult years that I learned it's possible to achieve a higher level of success for myself, which helped me to start pursuing what I wanted. Believing you can attain success and move forward towards the things you want in life is a great position to be in. I feel many people get stuck at this point, because they don't think they are good enough to go after what they want, or they make excuses like not having enough time or money to pursue their goal(s). Anything in this world is possible if you allow yourself to believe it is. Seek out others who have shared their story of challenges to get inspired.

THREE: Learn everything you can

I am a huge fan of books and self-education, because they have been a key driver to my own success. You will find successful people learning and educating themselves on what they need to be great, while foregoing the latest television sitcoms or participating in the drama circles at work. They take the time to learn a new skill and stay on top of what's happening in their field of interest. This is what separates successful people from average people. They continually learn and implement what other people won't.

There is a wealth of information you can find in books, and you should take advantage of this. There are additional resources on the internet provided the source is reliable. One of the reasons why I'm successful is that I learn as much as I can about what I do, so I can be a better version of myself and for those who interact with me. Others can count on me to provide the value and expertise. I know you can do the same.

FOUR: If I put in the work, I can and will succeed

If you fail to put in the work, nothing worthwhile will happen. Once you identify what you want, you should start a plan to work and make it happen. I have seen countless memes and articles about how the road to success is not a straight line, but a wavy and often out of whack path. Believe me, it is! Expecting it won't be easy will set you up to face the challenges head on, instead of being reactive to the struggles. Productive action taken daily will move you closer to your goals faster than anything else. Anyone can work hard and still be stuck where there at, which is why it's important to be doing the right work to move you forward in your career or business.

FIVE: I can learn any new skill

According to the Pew Research Center, the average adult reads 12 books per year, with half of that group reading only 4 books or less per year. The take away here is that you can easily stand out by seeking the information that will make you better and more refined in your career, or business.

You don't have to look far to gain knowledge in a new area, or a new skill set. You can find free or low cost education, eliminating the excuses that you can't afford to always be learning. For some, it's too easy to sit back and binge watch a television series, rather than taking a little time daily, weekly, monthly and yearly to learn a new skill set that could earn them more money, or advance them in their job. You can't get that type of return on investment from watching television.

What if learning a new skill increased how much you are worth to the marketplace? What if the new skill you learned turned you into a highly skilled individual with more options for opportunity or increased pay or both? Would it be easier for you to make the decision to learn? Would it entice you to spend the time to be highly educated on your craft? I would say so!

I can tell you that my life changed dramatically once I started seeking out new skills which have allowed me to be more valuable to my career. Seek out those who share their knowledge to help others become successful and make it your goal to revisit the basics to remain educated and inspired.

Is there somebody that is successful doing what you want to do or making the kind of income you want to make? If you answered yes, then the next step is to seek out what they are doing and what skills they have-then replicate their actions. Find out what you need to do, or get to be on that same success level, or higher, as them.

SIX: Get up fast after a failure

I have to admit, this piece of advice took me a long time to master. Getting up after a failure can be tough. No matter how successful you become, failure will still exist. It's a myth that successful people are without failure. How those that are successful view failure is much different from those who are not successful. Successful people view failure as a learning experience and not so much a failure. They learn from it and move on to do what they need to do. Unsuccessful people view failure as a mistake that can keep them in a holding pattern that they often can't get past. Some may even view failure as an opportunity to quit what they're doing. We must realize that when failure hits, it can be an opportunity to turn a negative into a positive. Approaching failure this way allows you to view the failure as an opportunity to learn from it.

Can you think of a time when you dealt with a company over an issue that arose? How did they react to your concern? If they reacted by solving your problem, then you may see that company in a greater light and remain loyal to them. If they didn't solve your problem or reacted to your concern poorly, then you may not give them any more business. You may even give them a bad review, or share with others how poorly they treated you. The lesson here is to turn that negative into a positive and get back to your pursuit of a successful life. Don't let failure stall you in your efforts to change the course of your sail.

SEVEN: Become more resilient in what you do

Building your resilience muscle is a great way to stay the course and not let what you perceive as failure keep you down for the count. By increasing your resilience, we will be stronger and react much better when failure hits.

I had the pleasure of being interviewed by Savio P. Clemente (The Human resolve) for Authority Magazine about this very topic. I'm proud to say that this interview was so well received it made the top editors list and was shared on Buzzfeed too!

Here is one of the questions I was asked:

How would you define resilience? What do you believe are the characteristics or traits of resilient people?

For me, resilience is when you get back up after every defeat with the same drive and energy that you started with. When we understand that failure is something that should not stall, or hinder, our efforts to achieve our goals, but simply a lesson we learned, it can help us bounce back faster and remain resilient. I feel being resilient is about not giving up on what you want just because of a setback. It's about keeping our eyes on the prize.

Having goals mixed with the confidence to go after them on a daily basis are the main characteristics of a resilient person. It's these characteristics that can breed success, because it keeps us moving forward. Resilient people tend to have thick skin as well.

They don't let many things get to them. When you expect things to be tough and go in with a winning attitude, it can lead to the wins we desire. Some people feel that things should be easier because they have a great idea they are chasing. While it's great to be excited about something, we need to understand that the road to success is a windy one and never a straight path.

As you just read, building up your resilience can play a huge part in whether or not you get back up and stay the course. Negative thinking will provide negative results.

Read the full interview on my website:
www.ItsAllAboutTheRealEstate.com/press

EIGHT: Decide now is the time and take action

You can read this entire book and gain all the knowledge you can to make a change in your life, but if you don't decide that you will make the change, nothing will happen. When your back is up against the wall, you should be inspired to make the choice to create a better life for yourself and those around you. That's what happened to me back in the day. I became fed up with where I was at professionally.

Remember, if you feel you are at rock bottom, then there's no place to go but up.

If you're fed up in your job or personal situation, make the decision to change things now. Take the first step and learn what you need to do to make that change. Does making a change involve signing up for that night class you've been putting off? Does it mean applying for a better position that is better for your needs? Do you have to sacrifice a weekend day to learn a new skill, or work on another opportunity or side hustle?

Taking action and doing the things that will put you on a path of where you want to be is key to overcoming self-doubt. When you decide to set the wheel in motion, you will realize you can get what you want.

Take that first step today!

"Inaction breeds doubt and fear. Action breeds confidence and courage. If you want to conquer fear, do not sit at home and think about it. Go out and get busy."

- Dale Carnegie

RECOGNIZING FEAR AND CONQUERING IT

We will experience fear when our brain communicates to us that we are in harm's way, real or thought up, and triggers a negative emotion in an effort to keep us 'safe'.

There are three types of fear that we should be aware of:

ONE: Rational Fear

Rational fear is when we are actually faced with a real threat. It's pretty clear how this comes about.

TWO: Primal Fear

Primal fear is when we have an innate fear programmed into our brains. Examples of this type of fear are having a phobia of snakes, spiders or anything else that sends chills down the spine. It could also be the fear of death, fear of being alone or deserted and/or fear of failure.

THREE: Irrational Fear

Irrational fear is the type of fear that doesn't make any logical sense and can vary depending on the person. Some examples of this is having a fear of clowns, fear of choking, fear of being humiliated, or being judged by others.

We will be diving deeper into irrational fear because I feel this is what many people experience in their life, especially as it pertains to the *force of average*.

Any type of fear, especially irrational fear, can keep you from moving forward towards doing something you want to do. If you are looking to make a change in your life that involves you doing something you have never done, you probably will experience the irrational fear telling you to not do the task. Your brain will come up with multiple excuses why you shouldn't do something new. For many, this is where the decision is made to not do whatever it is they were thinking of doing.

Irrational fear is a lot like self-doubt, only it involves the physical aspect of fear. Fear makes us not only doubt our decision to try something new, it communicates to us that we may be physically harmed, even though we won't. Allowing irrational fear to stop us from moving forward on a decision can keep us from changing our life for the better.

It's important to know how irrational fear can creep up on us and keep us from achieving what we want out of life. It's equally important to know how to conquer this type of fear.

Here are nine ways to fight irrational fear:

ONE: Recognize that it's irrational fear

Be able to recognize that your brain will throw irrational fear your way in an effort to protect you from doing something new or challenging. Knowing that this type of fear exists will give you a better chance of beating it.

TWO: Giver yourself a time out

Time outs aren't just a form of punishment for children, they can be a great way to give you the mental break you need to reassess what's going on. Giving yourself a time out will allow you to re-group your thinking and make a sound decision.

THREE: Face the fear head on

Facing your irrational fear head on will help you achieve what you want out of life. Once you recognize the fear exists, combat it with positive thinking and action. These two elements will make it easier to get past the fear effectively.

FOUR: Imagine what's the worst that will happen

Ask yourself *"What's the worst that will happen if I take action and ignore the fear that I'm having?"* Chances are nothing life threatening will occur, if you move forward against your fear.

FIVE: Now imagine what's the best that could happen

Now that you know what the worst thing that could happen is, ask yourself what's the best thing that could happen. Think of a potential positive outcome should you ignore your fear and take action towards doing the thing you want to do.

SIX: Talk it out

Talking things out, even if your alone, is a great way to get past your fear because it allows your brain to listen to the problem your having in an effort to make a right decision. It may sound silly, but try it to see if it works for you.

SEVEN: Don't try to be perfect, nobody is

Part of conquering fear is realizing that things will never be perfect and that all you can do is your best. When I realized that being a perfectionist is a huge waste of time, it made me feel much better about what I was doing. Nothing in life is perfect, so remember this when fear has you thinking that everything needs to be perfect.

EIGHT: Breathe

It's highly beneficial to take a deep breath and allow your body to respond to the fear you're having without causing a panic attack, which some people have been known to have. Take a minute to breath and give your body what it needs to conquer the fear.

NINE: Take action and move forward

Taking action moves you past the point of allowing fear to paralyze you in your tracks. You must move forward past the fear with swift action.

Now that you know that fear can be something that comes up without any logical reason, you will be better armed to conquer fear the next time it reveals itself. If you're having a hard time making a decision to do something new and challenging, just remember that it's only irrational fear keeping you from doing the great things you want to do in your life.

"Nobody needs to prove to anybody what they're worthy of, just the person that they look at in the mirror."

- *Picabo Street*

BELIEVING YOU ARE WORTHY

It's an absolute necessity to have a firm belief in yourself and that you are worthy of success. If you don't believe in what you are doing, or that you are worthy of achieving, then you will fail before you begin. It would be safe to say that many people haven't found the success they desire, because they didn't feel worthy of it. Maybe they never pursued success to begin with, because the proper belief system was not in place.

Whatever the reason, believing you are worthy of success can take things to a whole other level. It can mean the difference between having a great life, or having an average life.

Maybe you just want a better paying job, but you never took the first step to make that change, because you didn't feel that you deserved it. The result being you staying in the same dull spot you're in without advancing to a better position, or opportunity. This would not be the case if you had a strong belief in yourself.

People who are successful tend to believe they are worthy and even deserve it. They believe they are a racing supercar in a sea of domestics.

Here are 6 ways you can believe that you are worthy of success:

ONE: Take action and just do it

You probably know someone who seems to always be ready, aiming and aiming, only to never fire or take action! They go from one big idea to the next regenerating their short lived excitement each time. When you are looking to do something new, fear will want to step in and paralyze you. This combination of being paralyzed with the thought of not feeling worthy could lead you on a path towards nowhere fast. You must take action and realize that the task is something you can do, which will build your self worth quickly.

I have known salespeople who had the notion that they were not good enough at what they were selling to go after bigger and more profitable businesses. They allowed themselves to believe they are not worthy of bigger accounts, higher commissions and more recognition. This type of thinking caused them to not discover their true potential. Had they taken the first step towards getting in front of bigger customers, without over thinking it, they would have had one of the customers placing an order, or hiring their service.

Taking action is one of the best ways you can feel worthy of the success that is tied to what you want. Taking that first step will allow you to see what you are capable of without hesitation. Learning this tip will have you feeling inspired and ready to take the necessary action more often until you achieve the goal(s) you set for yourself.

I shared with you a great example of how some salespeople don't believe they are worthy of larger and more profitable commissions. Many salespeople spend years in the sales profession and never see big sales numbers, or they struggle monthly to hit their quota. This same advice can be applied to just about anyone who needs to feel worthy of taking action to get where they want to be. Take employees for example. An employee keeps complaining about their job, yet never takes action to find a better one, or make the job they have more appealing. Another employee wants to ask for a promotion, but never does, because they don't feel they are worthy.

Don't over think it. Just take the first step!

TWO: Build a support group around you

Take a look around and see who is the most supportive of you and build a network or support group that includes those people. Your support group needs to include people who will be very honest with you. Pure and honest feedback will allow you to make sound decisions on any form of action you are thinking of taking. It will also help you to be open about the feedback. You will never grow if you always think that you are doing the right things. Positive feedback will help you grow.

It also helps when the people in your group are more successful than you. When you hang with others who are on the level that you want to be, they will lift you up with their knowledge and wisdom and maybe even pure motivation. You never want to be the smartest person in the room because that won't expand your thinking. Not to mention you won't learn anything.

Surround yourself with helpful people who can help change your life.

THREE: Focus

I can tell you from my own efforts that having a strong focus plays a huge part in achieving the things you want out of life. Focus is probably one of the most overlooked areas of learning as well. When you project a laser focus on what you are doing, you won't have time to not feel worthy. Your sights will be aimed towards that big goal you set for yourself and you will be inspired by it. You should also be focusing on your smaller goals, because they can lead to the big goal(s) being achieved.

By having the proper focus, you won't over think taking that first step to believe you are worthy. No longer will you procrastinate or waste time because you have a new life to attain. You won't fall victim to drama, or any other time suck that will rob you of your success. You will be a focused warrior going into battle daily ready to win the war. You must remain focused on what your end result is and continue the course.

FOUR: Tune out your inner voice

Unless you are facing a real life danger that will physically hurt you, it's time to tune out your inner voice. You know the one I'm talking about. The little voice in your head that tells you that you shouldn't do something different, new, or challenging, because you may fail at it, or the one that states you are not good enough for any new opportunity that presents itself. Calling out your inner voice will allow you to build up the self-worth you need to take that first step. Your inner voice will provide you all the reasons why you shouldn't go after the big success or change the direction of your life to better favor you.

Understand that your inner voice does have the power to keep you where you're at in life, only if you allow it to. The next time your inner voice rears its ugly head, trying to sway you in the direction you don't want to go, recognize the voice is projecting false fear. When you have control of your inner voice, you will be able to tune it out and take the first step towards your goal(s).

FIVE: Change Your Negative thinking

One of the things you can do to feel worthy of success is to block out all your negative thoughts. With the right steps, you can accomplish this fairly easily. Blocking out the negative thoughts means you need to fill your head with positive information that will drive you to not only feel worthy of achieving, but you will be given the motivation to take the steps necessary to become a success.

One of the ways I block out the negativity is by listening to audio books and interviews of other successful people who are on the level I want to be on. It inspires me to learn how these people became successful. I love learning about how these people over-came hardships and challenges to become who they are today. I have been doing this for years and I love the benefits it provides.

To apply what I mean to a metaphor, it's like enjoying the benefits of drinking water verses drinking pop. At first the pop tastes so good, but then you experience all the negative things that it does to your body. When you drink water, you enjoy all the positive things it provides your body, such as natural energy and various health benefits.

The same goes for what we feed our mind.

If we take positive information into our mind daily, we gain the benefit of thinking mostly positive. We can also learn from others who have achieved success, which in turn inspires us to feel wor-thy, because someone who probably had a worse situation than us accomplished such great things, and so should you.

SIX: Enjoy the path you're currently on

It can become stressful to work towards creating your new life;

especially when you don't see the results as quickly as you hope. You put in the time and effort only to feel like you're seeing very little change, or no real change at all. You must remember that it takes time to make a great change, and it's important to have some fun and enjoy the path you are on. Even if you're not exactly where you want to be at the present moment, when you put the enjoyment of the journey you are on first, it could be the difference between getting burnt out, versus being productive and staying the course. Be sure to enjoy the process and the fact that you are trying to do something great for yourself. Remind yourself of why you want to change your life, achieve success and create more fulfillments in your work. Do this daily.

Early on in my career I thought that I could achieve success and then it would just stay with me forever. I felt that it was something that I would have with me forever.

This was certainly not the case.

I learned that I need to enjoy the journey towards success and that what I am doing so that I don't lose what I've achieved thus far. You must enjoy what path you are on to feel worthy and positive about what you're trying to do. Feeling this way means you won't dread your daily grind, or the stuff you have to do currently to get you towards your true path.

Even if you are in the beginning stages of changing your life, you must remind yourself that you are in the process of making a positive difference in your life. You can never own your success; you simply rent it daily through your focus and effort.

"You become like the five people you spend the most time with. Choose carefully"

- Jim Rohn

BIRDS OF A FEATHER FLOCK TOGETHER

William Turner once said *"Birds of a feather; flock together."* This quote couldn't be truer. It's very important to remember that you are similar to those you hang with. If you hang around others who make bad decisions, then you will make bad decisions. If you want to be a millionaire, then hang around other millionaires. If you are looking to be a loser, then hang around other losers. Actually, please don't hang around losers! You must be selective about who is in your circle of friends, or associates, because those around you will affect your thinking and actions.

Does this mean you can't have friends that are different than you? Of course not. It does mean that if you are looking to make big changes in your life and you have others around you that don't improve your way of thinking and living, then it's time for them to go. This may sound harsh, but ask yourself how important your goals are and how bad you want to make that positive change in your life. You can't afford to let others stop you from reaching your goals.

This advice might be hard to swallow for some of you, because you may have friends that you have known for years and you can't imagine them not being in your life. I get it. It can be hard to disassociate people from your life. Please keep in mind that this advice applies to those who are dragging you down like an anchor. This could also apply to giving attention to those who complain about their own lives-yet never making any change. At companies, negative people congregate by the water cooler, or break room, complaining about the boss, or work situation, often. They are the ones who aren't productive at all as they waste time gossiping about who is dating who, or that someone in the workplace they dislike.

You need to be selective about who you keep in your life so that you're not being held back and robbed of your true potential. Have no room in your life for those who spew negativity towards anyone who will listen. Make the decision to better your life by weeding out the drama and the whiners. You will be glad you did!

Still unsure of how you can increase the quality of your circle?

Here are three tips on how to hang around others who inspire you often

ONE: Locate like-minded people and groups

Seek out others who share similar interests as you and network with them. You can reach out to just about anyone with the help of the internet. Locate groups that focus on your interest(s) and join in on the conversation. Be sure to be a contributor as well. Talking with others about your interest(s) can really be a huge motivator and push you in the right direction. Remember that positivity is contagious as well. When you are around others who are going after goals and learning, it can be inspiring to be around them.

TWO: Let go of people who drain you

Let's face it. Negative people suck. They have a complaint about everything that exists and love to bring others down. They can also be the rain on your parade. Letting go of the negative people in your life will help keep your mind where it should be-on your path to greatness. Negative people will always be the ones who succumb to the *force of average*. I have seen people constantly give attention to negative people, as if they're mesmerized by them, even though they say they can't stand them. Don't let these people bring you down with them. I am drawn to people who have goals and ambitions for a better life, because I find it motivating. It drives me to keep improving my own life. They serve as a reminder that anything is possible. Negative people don't have that affect on me and they shouldn't towards you either. There should be no place in your life for negative people, so make the cuts today.

THREE: Surround yourself around people already successful in your area of interest

Do you know what you want your new life to be like? Seek out those who are doing what you want to be doing and make the connection. There is a great quote by James Keller that goes "*A candle loses nothing by lighting another candle.*" Many of the successful people I know are happy to help others become successful. They truly want to help those that want the help. Yet some people believe that high achievers are snotty, selfish and only care about themselves. Surrounding yourself with successful people will make all the difference. You should also work to be a beacon of hope for others, lifting them up whenever you can and never forgetting how you changed your own life for the better. Always be willing to help others.

Finding a suitable mentor could be a challenge, yet it can be a great way to hold yourself accountable to what goals you set for yourself. The key is to locate a mentor that you can communicate well with. Your mentor doesn't have to be someone you know either. A mentor could be a famous author, celebrity, life coach, or anyone else that is beneficial to keeping you on track. Think about it. Tony Robbins is one of the most foremost experts in personal development with almost everybody on the planet knowing who he is. Every day he has millions of people tapping into his words of wisdom so that they can create a better life for themselves. His programs are designed to hold those who buy into them accountable for their actions as they pursue their goals and desired life. This is proof that you don't have to personally know your mentor to have one.

The purpose of having a mentor is to have someone who holds you accountable to get your tasks done. As you search for your own mentor, make sure it is someone that motivates you to take action and separate yourself from the rest of the pack.

If you're meeting with an actual person you know, it's important to be humble and to recognize that you don't have all the answers. You are meeting with your mentor to bounce ideas off of them and to gain more knowledge about what you're doing. You should never approach a mentor with a know-it-all attitude, because you won't gain anything from it. You should always remain a student and learn as much as you can about whatever it is you do or want to do.

I just shared with you three tips on how to position yourself around those who motivate you and make you feel more confident to move forward. Make it your daily mission to be around people who inspire you to be the person you want to become. Negative people come with all sorts of headaches and drama, so it's important to dismiss them from your life. You won't have any time for negative people as you progress on your new journey.

"The trouble is, when a number, your age, becomes your identity, you've given away your power to choose your future."

- Richard J. Leider

AGE IS JUST A NUMBER

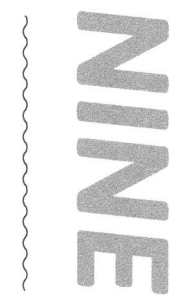

As I was preparing this section, I couldn't help but think of the inspirational story of how Harland Sanders aka The Colonel started his fast food empire in the early 1950's 'Kentucky Fried Chicken'. While it is disputed as to when the Colonel actually started the brand, he incorporated the name when he was 65 years old. The Colonel then traveled the USA looking to franchise his restaurants and spread the word outside of his home town about his delicious recipe for chicken and other side items. As you know, it was a huge success making Harland Sanders a wealthy man. Most importantly, he designed a life for himself that he truly loved living.

When you look at making a change in your life, you must never look at your age as a barrier. Your age is not a deciding factor in whether or not you need to change your life for the better. Age in itself is just a number that we use to give the world an idea of how much we have experienced-or not. Age is irrelevant to what you want to accomplish in your life. The story of Colonel Harland Sanders should be an inspiration to anyone who has a dream, goal, or vision-big or small. You should not use age as an excuse to not do better for yourself.

Would you want to be on your death bed wondering 'what if' you had only done this or that?

I don't want that.

Chances are you don't either. The pain of regret would probably outweigh having the pain of defeat.

"When you know what you want, and you want it badly enough, you will find a way to get it."

- *Jim Rohn*

KNOWING WHAT YOU WANT OUT OF LIFE

In my early 20's I was working for the weekend and dreading every Monday without knowing what I wanted out of life. I was caught up in the process of working hard and just getting through the days. I always thought maybe I should pursue something better, but I never really thought about chasing bigger opportunities. I would look for a slightly better job with a better title thinking that was the answer to my problem. It wasn't. I felt stuck working in my mundane job, while I was not earning much of a living.

I've seen people go the college route, earning their degrees and making a nice living doing something that they didn't mind. For me, I felt as though I was on a treadmill running in one spot, sweating and working my butt off for low pay without much to show for it. I would ask myself if this is what I was really meant for.

Was I going to be stuck in a dead end job all my life?

Was there any hope for me professionally, or would I have to settle for this average life?

Am I smart enough to make more money and have a career that I could love?

All these questions ran rampant throughout my mind.

When I came to the realization that I wanted more out of life, I began to make changes and push forward. I took the initiative and registered for college classes, leading me to earn my college degree. I started working at an entry level sales position where I gained the professional sales skills needed to be successful. I finally felt as though I figured out the path I wanted to take. It comes as a relief when you find something you enjoy and turn it into an opportunity to better your life. The more I progressed through my sales career, the more I learned about the importance of setting goals and knowing what you want out of life and where you want to be. Not knowing what you want, or not having goals, is like a ship without a sail. It's important to identify what you want out of life so that you can start to pursue a path that gets you closer to it.

Here are four tips on how to figure out what you want out of life:

ONE: Know what you don't want

This is an easier one to begin with, because most people know what they don't like, or don't want. For me, I didn't want to be stuck in a dead end job with no meaning, or no purpose. Can you think of something you dislike? Take some time to jot down the things you don't want to do and work backwards from there. Rule out everything you don't want to do in your current life and then identify what you do want to do in your newly designed life.

TWO: Plan for the week

Once you have an idea of what you want out of life, it's time to plan the actions needed to get you there. To help with this planning, grab a piece of paper, or a digital planner, where you can schedule your week(s) ahead of time. Even if it's only a couple of actions you can take, schedule it. Benjamin Franklin once said-"*If you fail to plan, then you are planning to fail.*" If you don't take the time to plan your days, you will wander around aimlessly not focused on what you need to be doing to get you closer towards your goal(s). Myself as an example, my day starts the night before with planning and review. I look at my calendar and take note of the most important tasks I need to accomplish in that day. I confirm that what I am doing makes sense and that it will be a day of actions that are necessary. Remember, preparation breeds success.

THREE: Find someone who you are envious of

Envy can be a huge motivator for you, if you harness it in a healthy way. For example, you're outside your home and you see someone down the street washing their new flashy car. You scroll through social media and you see a cute vacation picture posted by one of your friends from a place you've always wanted to go, or wouldn't mind going to. You think to yourself how you would love to get away for a vacation like that. While it would be easy to dwell and ponder over the idea of that not happening for you, you could instead let that be a motivator in your life. If you take the power of envy and allow it to push you to take the steps necessary to make more money or do those things you want, you will have empowered yourself to move forward. Don't think for a second that you can't obtain the nice things you want because you feel you are different than others. Because guess what? Everyone in this world is different. It's how it is.

This piece of advice is in no way meant to encourage you to keep up with the Joneses. It's simply fuel that can be used for your internal fire.

FOUR: Determine what really makes you happy

Happiness plays a huge role in your overall mood and whether or not you feel like achieving your goals. Ask yourself these questions. Do you know what makes you happy? Do you know how to be happy? Do you know what happiness looks like? Take a look at what you do and how you spend your time to determine what really makes you happy. If you're still unsure, then ask yourself these additional questions:

What makes you excited to get out of bed early?

When do you feel you are the happiest?

Am I spending my time on what is most valuable to me?

What am I grateful for?

What do I feel is going right in my life?

Am I more motivated by fear, or passion?

Grab a notepad and jot down your answers to these questions so that you can identify what truly makes you happy. Don't take this process lightly either. Spend some time brainstorming things you like and see how they can be tied to your goal setting for your better life. By defining what makes you happy, it will become easier to figure out the path you need to take to become happy in your personal and professional life. Knowing is half the battle.

"Setting goals is the first step in turning the invisible into the visible."

- *Tony Robbins*

HARNESS THE POWER OF GOAL SETTING

Every successful person that I know has set goals for themselves. The goals they set are short and long term objectives they want to achieve. It's important to set goals for yourself so that you have something to aim for as you work on your new life. It's not enough to just think of them, you need to be specific about what you want. Once you figure out what your specific goals are, write them down and attach a deadline to each one. This will allow you to excel over most people who have no goals at all.

One of the things I love about goal setting is that it gives us permission to daydream. It opens our mind to what is possible and provides clarity in our mission. When I look at what I want to accomplish daily, weekly, monthly and annually, I think about what my goals are for my business and personal life. I always review my goals, because it makes me feel like I am working on something that is truly mine. It provides me a target to aim for.

Once you figure out what your goals are, it's time to put pen to paper. Whether you want a new kitchen for your home, or you're trying to exceed your income goal for the year, write it down and keep it in a place where you can review it daily.

Here are two examples of how a specific goal reads:

Within 2 years I will have updated my kitchen with new quartz countertops and a ceramic tile backsplash with neutral grey paint.

By the end of 2022, I will have purchased a 2022 Ford F-150 with leather interior, a black paint job and a foldable bed cover.

You need to be as specific as you can when it comes to your goals. As you read each goal, you want them to appear possible and real.

Not sure how or where to keep your goals front and center?

Let's explore these five tips on keeping your goals close:

ONE: Get a binder and some clear pocket sheets to go in it

TWO: Print a picture of each of your goals placing each one in a sheet

THREE: Write, or type, a brief description of your goal below each picture. Add a specific deadline to each goal. i.e. I want to go to Disney world by December 2023.

FOUR: Put each goal sheet in a binder under its own category. Your categories could be Family, Money, Retirement, Career or Business etc. You get the idea.

FIVE: Keep your goal binder in a place where you can review it daily. Take it one step further and create a digital PDF of your goal binder and have it on your phone; although not as effective as a physical binder.

It's really that simple!

Are you looking to go on a vacation this year? Get a picture of your destination and add it to your binder. Looking to buy a new car? Put a picture of the make and model you want in your binder. Your goals should be in a place where you can easily review them to inspire you to go after what you want. Don't forget to add a deadline to each goal too! If these things stay bound up in your head, you will never be motivated to achieve the tasks to get you there.

Side note: *You must know that your goals may change as you progress throughout the year. It's still important to have them in front of you.*

Now that you know what you have to do to get your goals in

check, let's talk about how to go after them.

Here are three tips that will help you take daily action towards your goal(s):

ONE: Have a paper or digital calendar

My calendar changes often with revisions being made last minute. This is why I prefer a digital calendar. Some people prefer a paper calendar, or planner, which works great too. Before I even step foot outside my house, I check my calendar and review my plan for the day. I run through my calendar daily, weekly and monthly to ensure that what I need to get done is scheduled. Not having a daily plan will lead you to be unproductive, wandering through the day, procrastinating on getting things done. I know that if I follow my calendar, I will take action and get closer to achieving what I need to do to get to where I want to be. Having my calendar in front of me keeps me focused on what is important to me professionally and personally. No matter what I need to do, even if it's just picking up milk, it get's scheduled in my calendar.

You might learn that a paper calendar or planner is better for you, and that's ok. The important thing is to get a calendar going for yourself and use it all the time.

Does your kid have a soccer game or a birthday party to go to?

Put it in your calendar.

You have to follow up with a potential client on Monday?

Put it in your calendar.

You get the point.

The successful people that I know live and die by their calendar, and you should too. One of the reasons why I love my digital calendar is that I have access to it anywhere I go from my phone, or computer. This allows me to not miss anything important whether it's a meeting, or a family event. Imagine how much more organized your life will be and how much more you can get done when you start using a calendar.

Remember, the key is to actually use it!

TWO: Keep your goals in sight

Having your days, weeks and months organized will do you no good unless you take the initiative to complete those things. When you have your goals in sight and the tasks in your calendar, you will have the motivation to get those things completed. Motivation is something that has to be instilled into your mind daily to keep you driven to succeed. This is why I mentioned having your goals in a goal binder. You can have a full day planned, but if the change in weather makes you feel too lazy to do anything, then you have lost. Reminding yourself of your goals and what that future success will do for you is crucial to taking massive daily action. For me, I work hard whether it rains or snows. It just doesn't matter to me. My goals are in my sight and it drives me to go out and go after what I want in life. My goals act as little triggers that motivate me to do something.

THREE: Know how you are doing and track your progress

It's important to know how you are doing in your career or business. It's even more important to know how you are doing in life. Keeping track of the results of your daily actions will give you the information needed to tweak your planning to be more productive.

I believe that many people fall victim to the *force of average* because they don't take the actions necessary to change their life. I hate to admit that I have been guilty of this from time to time. A good sitcom or movie sounds better than reading a book, or learning a new skill. While it's certainly ok to do these things once in a while, the *force of average* can take hold and keep people in this spot; many times for the rest of their life. It's easy for us to slip into a routine that pushes our important tasks and learning to the side-eventually causing us to quit.

Taking daily action is what will separate you from the average. While I would like to think that I am naturally driven to succeed, I have to admit that I don't always feel like taking action. But in order to get to where I want to be in life and hit the goals I set for myself, I have to stay the course and take action. The same goes for you and your life. This doesn't mean that you can't take a day off. It does mean that you need to make the most of your time on the days you work and be productive.

Remember to follow your calendar and complete the tasks you have scheduled. Don't procrastinate on your calendar items, because you never know what task will lead to your next opportunity.

"I still sometimes feel like a loser kid in high school and I just have to pick myself up and tell myself that I'm a superstar every morning so that I can get through this day and be for my fans what they need for me to be."

- *Lady Gaga*

FEELING LIKE AN IMPOSTER? REALIZE IT'S A SYNDROME

If you have ever doubted your ability to do something, or felt as though you are a fraud in what you are currently doing, you may be suffering from something called the imposter syndrome. Many successful people have experienced this syndrome at some point in their career and life. The Imposter Syndrome is a syndrome that has many people feeling like an imposter or fraud towards what they are trying to do.

This syndrome can have you thinking that maybe you are a 'fake' or that you are not good enough to be considered an expert in your career or business. This syndrome can cause you to feel that you shouldn't take action, because you may be perceived poorly amongst others.

Here are some examples of what the imposter syndrome is and how it can affect people:

EXAMPLE ONE:

A recent high school graduate arrives at their new college of choice. As the student is walking through the campus and setting up their dorm, they suddenly feel like maybe they don't belong at this college. The student looks around at the other students and suddenly feels not as smart, or inadequate. The student begins questioning their ability to perform well at this college and even considering the decision to quit the school.

EXAMPLE TWO:

A professional decides to interview at another company in an effort to gain a more beneficial position with a higher income and learning opportunity. The professional meets with the interviewer and towards the end, is given an on the spot job offer. The professional considers what the offer is including pay and realizes that the pay is much less than they feel they are worth. However, the professional starts to have doubts about whether or not they should take the role. Doubt starts to take hold of the professionals mind, making them think that maybe they are not worth the higher pay that they were originally seeking. The professional decides to stay in their current role.

EXAMPLE THREE:

A worker has been at a large company for decades and has been offered a promotion as a Manager. At first the worker recognizes that the promotion would be a huge advancement, compared to what their current role is. After thinking it over, the worker starts to doubt that they could do the job. They ask themselves what would happen if they mess things up, or if they do something to make themselves, or the company, look bad. They decide against taking the promotion.

All three of these examples share one common thread, the imposter syndrome caused each person to doubt whether or not they deserve what was offered to them. When something great comes your way, you may get the feeling that it's over your head, or it's too good of an opportunity for you. Oftentimes people get stuck, never to overcome the imposter syndrome, keeping them in the same spot they're at.

On your journey to improving your life, you may get the feeling that you are not worthy of being successful, or that you are an imposter of some kind not capable of doing what it is you're being offered.

You need to recognize that this will happen in your life as you pursue your path towards greatness. You must remind yourself that you are capable of being a success and that it's your time to shine. Never allow yourself to fall victim to this syndrome because it will stall you in your efforts.

I had the pleasure of speaking with one of my colleagues who is proficient in the insurance industry. We had a nice conversation on his social media show where he brought up how the imposter syndrome could cause some people to cringe and slow down their journey towards success. He proceeded to ask me if I had ever felt this way in my endeavors and if so, how I overcame it.

I explained that as I started getting more mentions in the press and being featured in articles all over the world that I had experienced a slight amount of the imposter syndrome. Doubtful thoughts had run through my mind about whether or not I was good enough to be considered an expert in my field, and that I probably shouldn't be doing the work I was doing. Even though I had the credentials and expertise to back up my expertise, I let the imposter syndrome creep in. Since I taught myself about this syndrome and how to get past it, I overcame it fairly quick. Now that you know what The Imposter Syndrome is, you will need to recognize when it shows up to overcome it in your own life.

Here are three tips I have used to overcome The Imposter Syndrome:

ONE: Remind yourself that you are the expert

Everyone looking to achieve greater things in life will encounter the imposter syndrome at some point. When I had the slight encounter I just shared with you, I reminded myself I am an expert in my field and that I have great advice and real world insights to share. Knowing how to overcome this syndrome allowed me to not let things like self-doubt and hesitancy rob me of future opportunity. I looked back at all that I have accomplished and how far I had come. This made it easier for me to keep moving forward. You can apply the same techniques to overcome this syndrome.

TWO: Consult with others who believe in you

It's beneficial to consult with others who believe in you to gain that reassurance that you are on the right path and worthy of success. Having a solid circle of friends and/or colleagues can keep your mind on the right track. A positive network can remind you of how far you have come in your journey towards success and that you deserve the recognition you are given. Build up a network and reach out to them when you have any doubts about your effort or skill set. Always be willing to make adjustments to your network if needed.

THREE: Keep moving forward

One of the best tips I implement in my own life is to always be moving forward. I don't like to spend time doubting myself, or over thinking something, because I know it will stall my efforts. When you learn how to keep moving forward, you won't have time for things to keep you stagnant. You will learn how to make the fast decisions to keep you moving forward. Successful people move forward towards their goals without spending too much time on things that cause them to doubt their efforts. Successful people don't stay in one spot for too long, doubting their choices, or stalling their actions. They keep their eye on the prize and continue to work towards it. And so should you.

Now that you learned what the imposter syndrome is and how you can overcome it, you will be better prepared to overcome it when it happens in your life. Because someday it will happen.

"The first step towards getting somewhere is to decide that you are not going to stay where you are"

- *Chauncey Depew*

THE FLOOR IS NOT LAVA, TAKE THAT FIRST STEP

No matter how much you learn about creating a better life for yourself, you won't get anywhere unless you take that first step outside of what is called your comfort zone. The dictionary defines the term comfort zone as "a place or situation where one feels safe or at ease and without stress." Many people have gotten way too comfortable in this zone because it allows them to achieve less, or nothing, without the stress and anxiety of stepping out of this zone.

The comfort zone is a zone without fear of failure or failure itself, stress, familiarity, and lower levels of anxiety. This zone actually sounds like a peaceful place right? You know what the comfort zone doesn't have? It doesn't have ambition, opportunity, achievements and success, to name a few. The *force of average* we have been talking about loves to have people feel comfortable staying in this zone, never to ever take that first step out.

So why is it important to step out of your comfort zone? If you never take that first step outside your comfort zone, then nothing great will ever happen to you. If you allow yourself to remain in your comfort zone, you will limit your access to great opportunities, or new challenges, that could excel your income, career, business or anything else you are looking to gain. It becomes too easy to remain in the comfort zone because it feels like a safe place.

Many people will spend their entire lifetime in their comfort zone, settling for average and never making strides towards pursuing their full potential. The comfort zone will have them remaining a victim to the *force of average* convincing them that they can't make changes happen. In the short term, they may feel happy being in the comfort zone, telling themselves that it doesn't make sense to make a change in their life, because they are just fine where they're at. These are the same people who dread Monday and pray for the weekend to come. It's sad to say, but too many people are not doing what they love, or what they are passionate about day in and day out. For some people, they are perfectly fine living within their comfort zone. They are content with how there life is and they get by doing what they have always done.

By the way, this is perfectly fine if they are happy with this type of life. However, many aren't. I doubt you are one of those people, otherwise you would not be reading this book. You wouldn't have been intrigued by the title or the first words you read sparking your interest to learn how to make a change for a better life.

I mentioned earlier that many people complain about Monday, call Wednesday 'Hump Day' and love when Friday comes around. These are the same people who don't do anything to get out of the comfort zone, because they are content. The comfort zone won't allow you to grow as an individual or professional, nor will it allow you to achieve the goals you have in mind. If you are looking to beat the *force of average* and get out of this type of lifestyle, then it should be your priority to take the first step outside of it.

Stepping out of your comfort zone involves self reflection and figuring out what you really want out of life. It also takes courage to take that first step towards greatness. Without that first step, you will fall victim to your comfort zone as you go down a path of regret, while settling for average. When you learn to embrace the discomfort of first stepping out of your comfort zone, it will make you stronger minded, getting you closer to achieving the goals you have set for yourself. The more you step out of your comfort zone, the easier it will be, because you will be comfortable being outside of your comfort zone.

Here are three tips on how you can get out of your comfort zone:

ONE: Recognize that you are not happy with your life and you are in the comfort zone.

Are you stuck in your comfort zone? Are you just getting by every day and not driven to succeed at your current opportunity? Are you having fear of doing something different because you may get judged or feel out of place? When you realize that you are in your comfort zone and want to get out, it's time to recognize that something needs to be done. This leads to our next tip; taking the first step.

TWO: Take the first step to get out of the zone

Taking the first step out of your comfort zone is easier than you think. For example, could you learn a new skill to get that promotion you have been wanting? Could you walk into a larger opportunity and make that big sale that would make you look good to your peers? Could you bring more income to yourself and your family? Are you able to research a new opportunity in the evening after your boring day job? Take the time to do that instead of watching television or staring at your phone. Whatever your thing is that you want to do, you won't get out of your comfort zone, unless you commit to taking that first step.

THREE: Stay the course to stay out of the comfort zone

Once you have taken that first step out of your comfort zone, it's time to stay out of it for good. You can accomplish this by remaining focused on the next steps. Remember, many people stay in the comfort zone, only to achieve nothing new, or great, in their life. You must know that it's easy to slide back into your comfort zone, because of how tempting it is to remain average. You will be tempted to take the easy way out by doing the easier things that will not lead to success in your life. Remember, the *force of average* will be working against you to keep you in your comfort zone, so stay the course and strive to stay outside your zone.

I would like to share with you an interesting conversation I had about this very topic. I was speaking with someone about the comfort zone and how so many people seem destined to remain in it. I was asked if it's ok for a person to be comfortable remaining in this zone. They went on to share that many people are happy with the way their life is and not everyone is interested in being a huge success, or beating the *force of average*. Quite honestly, many people don't know what the *force of average* is. My opinion is that if someone chooses to stay in their comfort zone and not take any steps towards improving their life, they lose the right to complain about their days to anyone who will listen.

I went on to explain that if you have the ability to improve your life and you don't, then the fault lies on you. The other person was somewhat taken back by my words, but I explained that it's some hard hitting truth that many people need to hear. Don't let yourself be one of those people who complain about everything, yet do nothing about it. The world is filled with too many of these people.

Let me ask you this.

Do you know someone who complains daily about their boss, or whines about their paycheck not being enough, or that person who says their co-workers are out to get them? Perhaps you know the group of gossips that hover in the break room talking about the latest drama. Maybe it's someone in your household who comes home exhausted, spewing out details of how bad their day was and how badly they were treated, only it's more like a bad year considering how many times this occurs. Or maybe I just described you? Ouch! The people who complain about these things should be focusing on getting out of their comfort zone to better their situation and increase the quality of their days, not what everyone else is doing around them. Is it a company's fault that the pay is what it is? Maybe. Some would even say yes. I happen to disagree. When you realize it's up to you, and only you, to demand more for your life and forego blaming others for your problems, everything will become so much clearer. When you finally make the change needed for a better life, you will celebrate your days instead of complaining about them.

I was once that guy who would complain daily about my krappy pay and horrible bosses. I complained about the job I had and even some of the people around me. Blah, blah, blah. Come to think of it, I was probably annoying to be around. When I decided to get out of my comfort zone and pursue something different and more to my liking, it changed my life. I started seeing every day differently and with positivity, because I felt I had a purpose, because I did. We are responsible for ourselves and finding or creating our own opportunities. That oh so familiar comfort zone will rob you of this realization. Think about it. If you had a choice to either binge watch a popular show, or work on improving your life, which sounds better? Watching television sounds way more fun! This is why most people stay in the comfort zone all their lives. They don't ever think about the big picture of how they want their life to be, so they fail.

And then it happens.

One day you wake up realizing that you wasted away days, months, years, or a whole lifespan remaining in your comfort zone. Let's say you become terminally ill and as you lay on your deathbed, you are saying to yourself 'what if'. Over that period of time you told yourself you had more time to take that step and make a change, but you kept putting it off. You don't want to wake up one day old and grey without any time left for a choice to change your life, right?

Take that first step today!

"Be decisive. Right or wrong, make a decision. The road of life is paved with flat squirrels who couldn't make a decision."

- *Anonymous*

BECOMING MORE DECISIVE, A PERSON OF ACTION

Being decisive in your actions will allow you to move forward towards what you need to do at a faster pace without much, or any, hesitation. When you are more decisive in your actions, you won't fall victim to over thinking, which can keep you in one spot for too long. If you don't act and make up your mind on something you are pondering, you will have wasted too much time on that one thing. Being more decisive is not about convincing yourself that you are always right. It's about knowing that if you are wrong after making the decision, the outcome will be ok. A decisive person will make certain they have all the right information to make a solid decision; and they trust themselves to act on it.

So what does a decisive person actually do?

Someone who is decisive:

- makes plans based on previous decisions
- does not hesitate or avoid making a decision
- has a decision making process in place
- makes specific goals and sticks to them
- spends less time on smaller decisions
- is more open to change

These are just some of the traits that a decisive person has. Being decisive also means not being afraid to say no to the things that take your time away from working on your goals. Many times we fall into the trap of saying yes to others all too often, while never leaving time for ourselves. Being decisive will also help you avoid the *force of average* we talked about. Make the decision today to be more decisive in your daily work as well as your personal life.

Here are four tips on how to be more decisive:

ONE: Make small decisions fast

Learning to make decisions fast without over thinking can help you move faster towards your goals. Trust your instincts that you are making a smart decision and move on to the next task. If you still have doubts, use the process of elimination to narrow down your choices. Maybe even rely on past experiences to guide you through.

TWO: Stop overanalyzing

Analyzing too much information related to your decision can cause information paralysis. When you have doubt in your decision making skills, you tend to seek out more information only to be stuck in a holding pattern. You will do this over and over hoping for something to get you off that ledge of procrastination to make the decision. You have heard the definition of insanity right? Insanity is doing the same thing repeatedly expecting different results. Analyze the information you already have and make the choice. You should feel strong about the information you have and that you made the right decision. If you really get stuck here, then outsource or share your information with someone else who is qualified to guide you in the right direction.

THREE: Visualize the outcome

Ask yourself what you want the end goal to be after you have made the decision. What do you want to happen? Take a moment to visualize what you want the outcome to be after you have made your decision and then go after it. Do you want a better job? Visualize it. Do you want more money? Visualize it. Do you want to start that business? Visualize it. Visualize the outcome you seek in an effort to guide you towards the right choice.

FOUR: Don't try to be perfect

If you seek out perfection all the time, you will end up stalling. If you're working on something and you keep trying for perfection, it won't happen. Realize that nothing will ever be perfect and the only thing you can do is your best. Keep making progress and keep moving forward. Do you know someone who has a lot of great ideas, but doesn't execute on any of them? Do you know someone who complains about their job, but never seems to find the right one? If you wait around for things to be perfect, you will lose. Realize that perfection is an illusion that can never be caught.

"If you have no confidence in self, you are twice defeated in the race of life. With confidence, you have won even before you have started."

- Cicero

GAIN THE CONFIDENCE OF A BULL

When I was starting out in my sales profession, with little knowledge of what I was selling, I had to learn how to be conficent in what I was doing to win the sales I sought. I learned how to use my drive and ambition to go after success, so that I could get to where I wanted to be. This effort not only excelled me in my career, it also excelled the sales team I was a part of and the company that employed me.

I continued throughout my sales career display-ing the confidence necessary to go after the wins. This effort led me to sell more successfully than the majority of my colleagues. Having more confidence in yourself and what you have to offer can take you leaps and bounds ahead of your competition. Confi-dence doesn't just app.y to sales professionals either. Confidence can help bring success to just about anyone who is looking to level up.

Consider this.

You can have less training than the others, but if you are more confident in yourself and your work, you just might do better than them. It's important to build up your confidence to be effective in whatever you want to do. People love to interact with confident people, because they feel that they know what they are doing. With confidence, you build up that trust with others. Confident people tackle big things and aim to solve the problems they are given.

Do you want to be more confident?

Here are 10 ways to obtain and display more confidence:

ONE: Look at what you have already achieved

Sometimes we can be really hard on ourselves when we don't take the time to look at what we have already achieved in life. We may doubt ourselves, or think negative thoughts that could decrease our confidence level. Take note of all the things you have achieved thus far and keep it close by as a reminder that you have done great things. Remind yourself that you have come a long way.

TWO: Remind yourself of what you are good at

It can be easy to compare ourselves to others and think that they are better qualified or more experienced to get the success we want. You may feel inferior to those whom you have never even met, but you know they exist. By taking the time to remind yourself what you are good at and that you have a lot to offer, you can raise and keep your confidence level where it needs to be.

When someone asks me who I compete with, I explain that I compete only with the past version of myself. This means that you should only compete with your past actions and nobody else. Sure, you will want to know who your competitors are and what they are doing, but you should only strive to become better than who you were yesterday. Remind yourself what you are good at and how far you have come in your endeavors.

THREE: Set some goals and go after them

It's hard not to be confident and take action when you have goals in front of you daily. This is a great way to avoid having extra down time that could cause you to lose your confidence. Every day you will act on what you have planned, so you don't think about a lack of confidence. In other words, being too busy can be a life hack to be more confident and more productive.

FOUR: Dress for the part

It's been said that the clothes make the man. Well, the right clothes can also make just about anybody feel more confident. Dressing the part daily is a great way to boost your confidence, not to mention commanding the confidence from others to take you more seriously. Dressing good is a great way to project more confidence onto those who you interact with. Don't believe me? Go out into the world dressed down and see how people communicate with you. You will find that the treatment is much better when you dress for success. It's a shame this happens, but it does.

FIVE: Think positive to replace negative thoughts

Negative thoughts are nothing but a waste of time and energy. Replacing negative thoughts with positive ones will allow you to have a better day, week, month or year. Positive thoughts could lead to big ideas and better ways of dealing with negative situations or people. Any day of the week, people would rather deal with a positive person instead of a negative one. Think positively whenever you can to keep your confidence up.

SIX: Act positive

You just learned that thinking positive thoughts can benefit you daily. However, it's not enough to just read about positive things, you must act positive too. This is not about acting fake, or not being who you really are. Your positivity needs to be displayed through your actions on a daily basis for you to be the person you need to be. Acting positive when you interact with others will display a higher level of confidence that people will flock to; and you will win because of it.

SEVEN: Learn more about yourself

Generals never go into war without knowing their enemy, right? If your mind is telling you that you shouldn't be confident in your endeavors, it's time to find ways to axe that thinking. When you get to know yourself better, you will build up your confidence in a positive way. People who lack confidence are those who need to learn more about themselves to reveal their strengths and talents, allowing them to be more confident.

EIGHT: Be prepared or fail to those that are

Some say luck is what happens when preparation meets opportunity. When you are prepared for whatever opportunity comes your way, you have greater confidence, which will increase your chances of succeeding. People who don't prepare for an opportunity become unlucky. It's been my experience that one of the reasons why some people fail is because they lacked the information needed to be confident in what they're doing. I witnessed this in a former sales role as unprepared job candidates met with my sales manager and I.

During the interview, my manager would ask them why they would like to work with our company. This question was often met with an 'I don't know, because I didn't research the company prior to the interview' look on their face. Of course, these candidates never received a call back. The candidates that did come to the interview prepared were usually selected for a second interview.

Being prepared leads to confidence which leads to success.

NINE: Slow down your communication

Many people throw around as many words as possible, because they have a lack of confidence and feel nervous in what they are doing. You see this when people go to present in front of a large group, appearing to speed talk through their presentation or speech. This type of communication will get you nowhere fast. By slowing down your communication and taking in what the other person is saying, you will be cool, calm and collected. It's a much more effective way to solve someone's problems the right way.

TEN: Achieve smaller things to feel confident

I'm an advocate of gaining the smaller wins to get me to the bigger wins. By celebrating the smaller wins, you build your confidence level to where it should be. I reference the sales profession often, because that's who I am, although this method can be applied to any profession. If you're in sales, the best time to make another sale is right after the first sale, because you are riding high on the confidence from the first sale. The same goes for an employee who achieves small wins which they hope will lead to a larger win-maybe even that promotion.

Use the momentum from your newly gained confidence to take more confident actions towards more success.

"In every age there are plenty of people around to remind you what you cannot possibly do. Thank goodness, for these naysayers provide a priceless service: They spur us to achieve great things."

- Jerry Spinelli

OTHERS WILL RAIN ON YOUR PARADE, GRAB YOUR UMBRELLA

No matter how well you're doing in life, there will always be someone who doesn't get what you're doing. You know, the Debbie Downers. These types of people may even think that they are helping you make the right choice, yet they will fill your head with doubt about your new idea, or opportunity. In this book, we will refer to them as the 'naysayers'.

Naysayers are people who will rain on your parade intentionally, as well as unintentionally, in an effort to coach, or guide you. Naysayers do this mainly because they have no parade of their own. They don't have the vision of doing something new or exciting. For instance, naysayers will advise you to not start that business or apply for that new job because it's too risky or they don't believe in it, and you shouldn't either.

Naysayers will go on to point out everything that could go wrong if you make the wrong choice, leaving you to feel unsure about making your decision for yourself. This is only achieved if you allow them to affect your decision.

Unfortunately, naysayers are a cancer that can take the form of co-workers, friends, spouse, or even family. Sure, they probably don't feel that they're intentionally sabotaging your efforts, or doing you any harm by offering you their opinion. They may feel that they are advising you towards the right path, because of how they feel, or how they would react to the same decision.

One of the ways you can combat this is by asking yourself if what you are about to do is beneficial and enjoyable to you? Will your decision benefit your life and maybe those around you? Are you dead set on making the choice to try the new idea, even if you receive advice against it? When you come to terms that you don't need the approval of others to do what you want, you will experience a type of peace that will allow yourself to move forward on potential opportunities. You won't allow yourself to be hung up on someone's opinion, because you will have made the decision for yourself.

You still might think you need the opinion of others before you consider starting something new. And that's ok. But I would debate that while it's ok to ask for someone's opinion or advice, you should not allow that to be the final say in what you do. You should never let others be the decider of your path, because that could potentially keep you in one place. You should also consider whether or not they are a good source to provide you the advice you seek. If you are looking at starting a side business and you ask someone who is an employee their advice, chances are you won't get applicable advice.

When seeking out advice from others, make sure that those people are doing what you want to do, or that they are at least knowledgeable in the area. Learning how to make decisions on your own is a part of gaining success. If you rely too much on the wrong people, it will hinder your efforts. Remember, many people have fallen victim to the *force of average* because they've allowed people to decide their life choices for them, so choose your experts wisely.

Here are ten ways to ignore the naysayers:

ONE: Define your dream to ignite your flame

Defining what your dream is and knowing what that looks like could put you in a powerful position filled with ambition and drive. When you define what that is for you, you will be unstoppable. You will tune out those who tell you what you should, or shouldn't, do. Defining your dream will ignite the flame you need to pursue it, no matter what.

TWO: Fight your internal naysayer

The naysayers aren't just people who fill your head with reasons why you shouldn't make changes in your life. There is an internal naysayer right between your own ears giving you reasons to not do something. While you will experience naysayers out in the world, the real battle begins with the one inside you. You probably know what I'm talking about. That voice in your head that tells you that you shouldn't take chances, or make a change in your life, because it won't work out. Make it your daily mission to ignore your internal naysayer on your path towards doing what you truly want to do.

THREE: Take some risks

If you're trying to do something new, you have to be willing to take some risks, big or small. Our brain has a natural state to protect us from certain things appearing dangerous; or fearful. When this happens, you need to know how to get past that cautionary alert by asking yourself how dangerous the task really is. In the sales industry, I've seen many salespeople have a fear of making the calls necessary to move their sales upward. They hesitate to pick up the phone and dial, or knock on that door, because they only picture the potential negative outcome. If you ask yourself how bad the outcome could really be, you could get past this fear and take the risk. Too often people get hung up and assume the outcome will be worse than it will be. Don't be afraid to take risks to move closer to achieving success. Ask yourself *"What's the best that could happen?"*

FOUR: Don't overshare your plan

There will be times where you will have excitement about a new idea, or opportunity and you will want to take to the rooftops to share your new plan to anyone who will listen. You will feel compelled to seek the advice of others who are not qualified to provide advice in what you want to do. The problem lies in the fact that not everyone will be as excited about your new idea, or opportunity, as you are. In fact, most won't show much excitement at all. You will face the naysayers telling you it's not the right thing to do. You will have others raining on your parade, because they don't want you to do better than them in life. Believe me, these people are not in short supply. What I recommend is creating a small and trusted network of people who can give you their qualified opinion to provide you a better idea of whether or not it makes sense to make your move. Notice I said your move. Ultimately, you should always make the final decision for yourself.

FIVE: Hang around some positive people

Nothing can halt your dream faster than negative thoughts and negative people. I can't tell you enough how important it is to hang around those that inspire you and share a common thread. This is not to say that you should hang around people who are exactly like you, that would be nonsense. You want to surround yourself with a diverse group of people to provide you different opinions and viewpoints that you can learn from. At all costs, avoid the Debbie downers, or the Loser Larry's. Negative people always have a problem for everything and they will drain your energy by filling your head with doubt and discouragement. Positive people will mostly have positive thoughts to share with you.

SIX: Expect resistance; Then move on

They say nothing that's worth having comes easy. And if success was easy to achieve, everybody would be successful. Targeting success is no different. You will face fierce competition, rejection, criticism, negativity, failure and others who don't see your vision the way you do. When you come face to face with these challenges, you will have a better chance of getting past them if you have resilience. By recognizing that this will happen no matter how much drive, ambition and skills you have, you will be better prepared for it. By the way, when you win, it makes it so much more worth it!

SEVEN: Consider failure as a learning opportunity

There was a time where I thought failure was a mistake I made, or an indicator that I did something wrong. When I learned that failure is only a slight setback, and that I shouldn't stay down for the count, it opened up a whole new level of thinking for me. Even to this day, I make it a daily game to fail as many times as I can. For every sale I have won, I failed plenty. For every press feature I was in, I probably pitched several that went unnoticed. I'm a firm believer that there are no failures, only learning opportunities. Condition your mind to accept failure as an opportunity to get you closer to your goals, and not a roadblock on the path towards your success.

EIGHT: Keep taking daily action

It's easy to allow ourselves to over think things and not take the action needed to move us forward. One of the ways I keep growing my business is by taking daily action; no matter how I feel. I know there will be good and bad days no matter how much I love what I do. The same goes for you. You will experience days where you just wake up not feeling ready to tackle things. You may even experience some doubt about what you are about to do that day. The solution is to take daily action, eliminate over thinking things, and to keep yourself busy. Apply this method to your life and you will increase your chances of success. Just make sure you are doing the right actions!

NINE: Consider the source of the naysayer

When you come face to face with a naysayer, you must consider exactly who they are. Let's say you decide to become a lawyer and you get some advice from someone who isn't one, or has no clue about what that entails, chances are their advice will not be appropriate for you. Warren Buffet once said *"Wall Street is the only place that people ride to in a Rolls Royce to get advice from those who take the subway."* You must never listen to those who are not qualified to give you advice. Seek out people who are experienced in what you want to do.

TEN: Actually ignore the naysayers

Now that you know how to ignore the naysayers, it's time to actually do so. Never let naysayers get into your thinking with their advice and wreck your chances at success. Be strong minded and keep your plan in place with your end goal in sight to get your hands on the success you seek. It won't be easy, but practice makes perfect when you work on this daily.

"Your most important priority is the one thing you can do right now that will help you achieve what matters most to you."

- Gary W. Keller

BECOME GREAT AT ONE THING, NOT AN EXPERT AT EVERYTHING

I will never forget reading the book 'The One Thing' by Gary Keller. In Gary's book, he outlines the importance of being great at one thing and not dividing your attention a bunch of different ways. He goes on to state that it's important to dominate one area of expertise to be known as an expert in that area. This doesn't mean that you shouldn't do multiple things in life. It does mean that we should be paying attention to how much time and energy we focus trying to be successful at too many things at the same time.

I've met many successful people who started off becoming great in one area before they branched off into other things successfully. By focusing on becoming great at one thing in the beginning, you can put in the effort and energy it takes to be great at it.

It's important to be 100% committed to the one thing you do. This will allow you to dominate and win success without having anything else distracting you. The great thing about success is that it requires a commitment that can challenge you to do new things. It doesn't matter what field you're in, or what you want to do, you should be committed and all in. Successful people are committed to making success happen for themselves and others.

"Formal education will make you a living. Self-education will make you a fortune."

- *Jim Rohn*

SELF-EDUCATION IS THE SECRET TO SUCCESS

I'm a firm believer that having an education is one of the keys to success. After all, if we don't learn anything, then how are we supposed to do something, right? How will we be proficient in something if we don't learn? Having the education to back up your expertise is crucial when striving to be successful. This is not to say that all education should come from a classroom, or a formal setting. I can tell you first hand that while I hold a college degree, it's what I learned outside of the classroom that took my career to new heights.

This is not in any way knocking a formal education, because that's important to have. It's simply a reminder that you need to be learning all the time if you want to be successful and beat the *force of average*. You must arm yourself with the skills necessary to win against your competition, as well as the past version of yourself.

I know from personal experience that self education can change your life for the better. You can seek out the proper information from millions of resources on any given topic you choose. It's also easy to consume information on your own terms, from podcasts, to audio books, to printed material. What you need to decide is whether or not you will take advantage of these resources and consume them to be skillful in what you do, or want to do.

Ask yourself these questions:

Are you willing to dive into this type of education to better yourself, your life and your future?

Are you willing to put in the hours of reading and learning necessary to have a competitive edge?

Some people will come up with an excuse or two about how they don't have time to learn something new that could excel them in their career or business. While that is a common excuse, it's also the easiest to overcome. What if you swapped hours of watching television with hours of reading? What if instead of listening to the radio in your car, you listened to an audio book? You can replace all these time sucks with learning opportunities that you can benefit from, if you choose to.

When you commit to self educating yourself and increasing your skill set, you will not only start to see a difference in your life, others will start to take notice of what you're doing as well. At first it might be the small subtle changes you've made at work, or in your personal life. As you progress further to educate yourself, the benefits will become more profound.

When I decided to make a change in my life, I researched different careers I had an interest in. I read books and took courses related to the path I wanted to take. Everything we need to learn is within our reach. When you start seeing the benefits of learning, you will become infatuated with it. You won't leave your house unless you have something educational playing in your car, or on your walk. Learning new things will consume your mind day and night for the better. You can apply this energy towards researching some paths you want to take for your life. Learning is something that provides many rewards. But don't stop there! You need to apply these new ideas and skills towards your career, or business. Never stray from the books, or stop taking the courses once you start gaining success, because they can offer so much.

I read a study somewhere that about 42% of college graduates never read another full book after they graduate. How can this be? This is one way to allow the *force of average* to keep you in one spot. It should always be on top of your priority list to learn new things. I can personally account for most of my success being tied to reading about other successful people.

Consider that the majority of highly successful people read

at least a dozen books a year. What does this tell you? Learning makes sense, and dollars!

When you decide that every day will be a day of action, things will start to happen for you. If you're in a dead end job, maybe you take a course around your current job schedule to learn a new skill that's in demand. Maybe you listen to an audio book on a topic that inspires you to apply for a better opportunity. There are so many ways to improve your skill set to get you into better opportunities-once you decide today is the day.

I just shared with you some great reasons how self education can change your life. Here is a warning though; this may result in less time watching TV, or streaming movies on Netflix. That's ok, because after all, you are changing your life here!

Here are four ways you can make self-education work for you.

ONE: Figure out what you want to learn more about

Self-education is a great way to increase your skills and transform you into the expert, or person you want to be. Once you figure out what topics will get you further along in your career, or business, it can be advantageous. Many people, including much of your competition, probably aren't educating themselves on what they do. They may even think they know everything there is to know about their profession. Their assumption will help you stand out in your space as you blaze a path past those who don't self-educate. Education in general will give you the tools necessary to be great at your craft.

TWO: Seek out others who inspire you

Many times people think of the word education as a boring class where they sit and daydream throughout the course, not really showing interest in the topic being discussed. The good news is that this is not true, at least when it comes to self-education. When you seek out information to educate yourself on a specific topic, you need to figure out who you would enjoy learning from.

Could you learn from someone who communicates well through their videos, courses, audio books or clips? Is there a personality that vibes with you making the information more enjoyable to consume? This would certainly make learning something more enjoyable, making you want to learn even more.

Educating yourself doesn't have to be a boring task. It can be fun and done on your own terms.

When I first learned of the benefits of self education, I sought out various topics online and at the local bookstore. I spent hours looking into different experts and content creators to find some-one that I found interesting. While I'm always open to learning new things from new experts I come across, I tend to have a hand-ful of experts I count on to keep me in the know. Find who is best for you and absorb their content as much as you can.

THREE: Figure out what medium works best for you

In this modern digital age, there are so many choices to choose from when it comes to how you want to learn. You have podcasts, digital and audio books, blogs, videos and other ways of giving us the option to learn how we feel most comfortable. With all these platforms available to us, there is no excuse to not be learning. Personally, I'm on the road often, which has me choosing audio books as a source of learning and inspiration; although my favorite way to learn something new is through a printed book.

While this process of learning requires time set aside, it's one I truly enjoy. Choose what medium works best for you and start implementing learning into your routine.

FOUR: Calculate how much time you can spend learning something

When you commit to adding self-education in your life, you can make the time to learn at your leisure. As I mentioned earlier, there are multiple platforms offering a ton of ways to learn a topic of your choosing. You could listen to an audio book, or podcast, while doing chores around the house, or driving in your car. You could read a book instead of binge watching the latest television show. You could watch a video on your lunch break, in between appointments or before bed.

There are many ways to take in the information we need to be more successful. The best part, your competition probably isn't doing any of these things.

Learning something new doesn't have to be just about your career or business. You could sign up for that cooking class you've always wanted to take, or join a group of like-minded people that hover around a topic you love, or join a fundraising effort that leaves you feeling inspired, because you have helped others. Deciding to learn something new can help transform your life into one that you truly enjoy.

"He who chooses to be a master never does 'just enough' to get by - nor does he cut corners or attempt to cheat the system"

- James Arthur Ray

NEVER CUT CORNERS IN ANYTHING YOU DO

I'm sure you know at least one person who likes to cut corners to get the job or task completed. It could be the contractor you hired to do some work on your home, the mechanic who said your car was fixed and it's not, or maybe it's the person you asked for help locating an item in the store and they gave you a series of directions, instead of escorting you to the item's location.

To cut corners means to ignore the risks that are, or could, be present, lying, or covering up problems, or failing to perform the job in an ethical manner. Cutting corners also means you do your job, career, business, or task half ass. People who cut corners hope to get to their end result faster by doing less than expected. The problem with cutting corners is that it affects you, as well as others, in a negative way.

At any stage of your life, you never want to cut corners to try to get further ahead. Not only will this type of behavior spread like wildfire, developing a bad reputation for yourself, it can lead to bad habits in your work. Successful people avoid cutting corners and doing anything that would jeopardize their job, or reputation, or both.

Here are 3 ways to avoid the temptation to cut corners:

ONE: Identify the risks involved

Ask yourself if any risks are involved if you are about to do something with less effort, or not meeting the expectations of the other person(s). If you are not meeting the full expectations of what someone else expects of you, then it's not worth the risk. By the way, there is always a risk involved.

TWO: Consider your environment and who it will affect

If you cut corners in any given area, how will that impact your environment, or those involved in your decision? Will someone else get hurt by your choice? Will it put you in a negative spotlight? Even if these things don't directly affect you, it's in good judgment to do the right thing anyways.

THREE: Will cutting corners affect your success?

Cutting corners cannot only affect others, but it could affect you directly. If you are serious about going after the success you want, you need to make sure that you are applying everything you have to becoming successful, and stay that way.

Consider this example:

Let's say someone runs a small business and they are having a pretty good year. Sales are up and they feel pretty good about the direction their business is going. Now let's say the small business owner failed to keep track of his expenses properly, or failed to pay the government their share of taxes. This is an area where the business owner cut corners, because he felt good in other areas of the business.

Cutting corners like this could mean this business owner gets drowned in back taxes, late fees and other negative effects the owner never considered. Even worse, the business owner lays off his employees, because of his decision to cut corners. One day the IRS comes knocking and seizes everything the business owner has, because he fell too far behind. Had this business owner took the time to do everything the way it should have been done and not cut corners, he would have been in a better position.

Never allow yourself to cut corners if you want to have long term success.

"Do not judge me by my success, judge me by how many times I fell down and got back up again."

- *Nelson Mandela*

BUILD RESILIENCE TO GET THROUGH THE TOUGH TIMES

It's a common misconception that most successful people never experience tough times, because their success makes things easier to deal with as though success and money solve all of life's problems. The truth is, no matter how happy, successful, or rich you are in life, or how much motivation and inspiration you have, everybody will be faced with challenging times that must be overcome to become, or remain, successful. Just because someone has gained the success they sought doesn't mean that tough times didn't, or won't, come their way. The key differentiator between resilient and non resilient people is how they handle the challenging moment(s).

Those who seem to have it all have learned to deal with tougher times by building their resilience muscle to face whatever life throws their way. Again, this doesn't mean that successful people don't experience hard times, or deal with issues easier. It means that the skill of building and having resilience is strong enough to get them through the tough patches with less effort. Knowing how to become more resilient could make a huge difference in how you deal with your own tough times.

I would like to share with you parts of an interview I had with **Savio P. Clemente** from The Human Resolve for Authority Magazine. We discussed this very topic about building resilience through tough times and how people can build up their resilience to make tough times easier to pass through. This is an interview that went viral, due to the importance of this topic.

Savio P. Clemente: We would like to explore and flesh out the trait of resilience. How would you define resilience? What do you believe are the characteristics or traits of resilient people?

Jason Gelios: For me, resilience is when you get back up after every defeat with the same drive and energy that you started with. When we understand that failure is something that should not stall, or hinder, our efforts to achieve our goals, but simply a lesson we learned, it can help us bounce back faster and remain resilient. I feel being resilient is about not giving up on what you want just because of a setback. It's about keeping our eyes on the prize.

Having goals mixed with the confidence to go after them on a daily basis are the main characteristics of a resilient person. It is these characteristics that can breed success because it keeps us moving forward. Resilient people tend to have thick skin as well. They don't let many things get to them. When you expect things to be tough and go in with a winning attitude, it can lead to the wins we desire. Some people feel that things should be easier, because they have a great idea they are chasing. While it's great to be excited about something, we need to understand that the road to success is a windy one and never a straight path.

Savio P. Clemente: Courage is often likened to resilience. In your opinion how is courage both similar and different to resilience?

Jason Gelios: I agree that courage does play a huge part in being resilient. When you have the courage to move forward and not let anything keep you down for long, it's empowering. When we look at how a soldier prepares for battle, it can put things into perspective. A soldier builds up the courage and skills to be resilient throughout all the elements they face. They are taught to adapt and overcome. Courage contributes to resilience because it offers the same principles.

There is some difference between courage and resilience in that resilience applies more to our mental state while courage applies to more of our physical state. Having resilience means we are stronger and we get past tough times mentally. Courage allows us to get past those tough times, but physically. Having both courage and resilience makes a great combination that can get us past anything life throws our way.

Savio P. Clemente: Has there ever been a time that someone told you something was impossible, but you did it anyway? Can you share the story with us?

Jason Gelios: *One particular time stands out where I had started at a major textile company as an outside sales person. Shortly after being introduced to the sales team, I was candidly speaking with a couple salespeople who shared with me that there top sales guy was impossible for them to beat. They had been attempting to dethrone him for the past year or so with no luck. They shared with me that no matter how hard they tried, they were unable to gain that number one spot. Having this conversation made me really want to take the number one spot. I had to prove to myself that I could accomplish this feat.*

I remember taking in all the product knowledge I could about what I was selling and figuring out what this top sales person was doing to be successful in his role. Within 6 months of deciding my goal, I surpassed him and not only took the throne of top sales representative, but also became the top representative in the region spanning three states. It was a great feeling because I had been told it was impossible after sharing my vision with the sales team. In the time I was working towards the top title in the office, I implemented everything I had learned about sales, product information and time management skills to become the top guy. I accredit staying resilient and having the courage to achieve that success as major reasons why I achieved my goal.

Savio P. Clemente: Did you have a time in your life where you

had one of your greatest setbacks, but you bounced back from it stronger than ever? Can you share that story with us?

Jason Gelios: One of my biggest setbacks was losing my position at a major company when I was number one on the board. It was a huge shock to me and even caught me off guard. I remember driving home after I had been let go wondering how I was going to rebound from this situation. Come to find out, it was a real eye opener. I reminded myself that I needed to be resilient and keep moving forward towards what I want out of life. It was a huge setback that taught me a lot about focusing on the bigger goals I had. Sometimes the vehicle to get us to where we want to go will change, but we should not be deterred from what we want when a setback happens.

Savio P. Clemente: How have you cultivated resilience throughout your life? Did you have any experiences growing up that have contributed to building your resiliency? Can you share a story?

Jason Gelios: Throughout my childhood, I had dealt with a speech impediment that made times tough. I dealt with kids mocking me and friends finishing my sentences, because I barely did it on my own. Despite all those challenges, I never wanted pity or sympathy. I kept being me and lived my life. I had a small group of friends that I felt understood me and we got along great.

While I had what I feel was a good childhood, I would be lying if I said my school life was something I would like to relive. Going through those times forced me to be resilient and courageous to *get me through the rough times. One of the ways I did this was to remind myself of why people act the way they do. I told myself that if those people were that low to throw insults at another person, then they must really be miserable in their own life. Learning and remembering this piece of advice really helped me through those hard times. It continues to play a huge part in my adult life and success in business.*

We must not allow others to dictate how we live our life and we must never allow ourselves to stay down for the count. It's important to apply resilience and courage to get through the times that can make us feel like failures. After all, a failure is just a learning opportunity that we should embrace and learn from.

Savio P. Clemente: Resilience is like a muscle that can be strengthened. In your opinion, what are 5 steps that someone can take to become more resilient? Please share a story or an example for each.

Jason Gelios: *The first step in building our resilience muscle is knowing what we have to offer and learning what our 'Why' is. When you know what you offer and why you go out and do what you do on a daily basis, it can add tremendous strength to our resilience muscle. One way to do this is to do some soul searching and actually write down your 'Why'. For me, it's family and personal growth. If I don't put maximum effort into everything I do, I feel like I am failing my family. Knowing my 'Why' and reminding myself of it daily keeps me resilient at times when I need it the most. In addition, knowing what we have to offer and feeling* strongly about it can really keep your resilience up, because that confidence will keep you going in the right direction.

Second, I would say stepping out of our comfort zones is a great way to build up resilience. I make it a daily goal to do something that makes me feel uncomfortable; within reason. Nothing great happens in our comfort zone, yet so many people get stuck in this zone, because it feels safe to them. I can tell you first hand that when we step out of our comfort zone, not only will we overcome our personal fears, but we will be even more resilient in our endeavors. I encourage everyone to do what makes them feel uncomfortable.

Third, we need to stop over thinking the situation. I hate to admit it, but I still struggle with this one. It's easy to get tied up on something that happened that maybe made us feel like a failure, or caused us to doubt ourselves. Over thinking what happened and replaying the situation is a waste of time, effort and potential. Over thinking can keep us stuck in that past moment and rob us of future opportunity. If we decide not to over think what happened and remember to move on from it, we can be leaps and bounds ahead in building resilience for ourselves.

Fourth, take a step back and breathe. Failure is never a fatal catastrophe-nor is it a brick wall that stops us in our tracks. Taking the time to breathe and briefly looking at the past experience can help us realize that we can move forward faster with the resilience we need to do the great things we seek. Failing to breathe and allow ourselves to move forward will not make us the resil-

ient person we need to be.

Five, find a way to laugh. Laughter is my favorite way to stay resilient, because I love the effects of comedy. No matter how bad a situation get's, or how sour we feel towards something, joy is always found in laughter. I love to push off stress by playing short comedy clips to put me in a better mood. Finding things that make you laugh hysterically can really change your mind set for the better.

- End of interview

As you just read, it's important to become resilient and courageous to get through the tough times that will come your way. Recognizing that there are no problems, only opportunities to provide solutions, will allow you to approach these obstacles with the resilience you need. By tapping into your resilience muscle, you will be stronger then you have ever been and nothing will keep you down for the count. This is what separates the successful from the unsuccessful, knowing how to get back on your feet faster after a setback.

"Great things are not done by impulse, but by a series of small things brought together."

- *Vincent Van Gogh*

SMALL STEPS LEAD TO BIG SUCCESSES

I have spoken to many people who felt they needed to take huge steps, or risks, to achieve the level of success they wanted for their life. They interpret successful people as those who got their success by taking on huge risks either with time or money, or both. They go on to share that they would probably gain success in their own life if they could only do the same.

I'm here to tell you this is not true.

If you tell yourself that it takes big moves to become a big success, or that you need to be in a different situation than the one you're in to go after what you want, then you have already failed before you even start. Making these assumptions could rob you of your true potential and keep you where you are at. You must find ways of overcoming these assumptions that exist in your head so that you can make the moves necessary to get you closer to your own success. It's imperative to you beating the *force of average!*

Oftentimes people will pay too much attention to these assumptions or doubts, allowing them to override our decision making ability. If you are looking to change your life for the better, you need to tune out these assumptions and move forward towards the action(s) you need to take.

The good news is that there are ways of doing this, which I'm about to share with you.

Here are seven ways to avoid making assumptions:

ONE: Be aware that assumptions exist

Half the battle is being aware of when assumptions cross your path, knowing when these arise, and taking the actions to overcome them. Recognize that assumptions will happen and get over them fast. We always have a better chance of overcoming something if we have awareness it exists.

TWO: Ask yourself the right questions

If you become faced with one or more assumptions, which you will, ask yourself how true it really is. Attempt to validate the assumption to see how serious you should take it. Chances are the assumption is not really valid, allowing you to move on past it.

Here's something you should know. All assumptions are false, which is why they are assumptions. Assumptions happen when we assume we know something about something completely based on false information. We see this when we have fear about something we are considering doing. Fear in itself is false evidence appearing real, and assumptions are no different.

THREE: Ask yourself what's the worst that can happen

Say you are scrolling through the job boards and you notice an available position within a company that you have wanted to work with, being a better opportunity for you. As you scroll further towards the job description, you suddenly start having an assumption or two run through your mind that you are not good enough for this position. You tell yourself that if you apply for the role, you probably won't get picked and that it will be a waste of your time. You decide to pass on applying for the role.

If you choose to ignore the assumption(s) and take the first step, what's the worst that could happen to you? Will you become physically injured, or even die? Probably not. After all, the worst the company could say is no. Or maybe they say yes! You will never know, unless you choose to get past that assumption.

By asking yourself what's the worst that can happen if you break through the assumption and do the thing you want to do, you discover a better way towards the chances of a positive result. And if you do this often, you increase your chances of gaining success.

Here's a couple more examples of what I mean:

If you're in a sales position and you assume that a potential client is not interested in what you have to offer, is it better to sit back and assume they won't buy from you? Or is it better to move past the assumption and see what the result will be?

Let's say you are a student in school and you forgot to turn in an assignment to your teacher. There was a deadline in place that you completely missed. Should you apologize and ask the teacher if they will still accept the assignment, maybe at a lower grade? Or should you accept the fact that the assignment deadline has passed and take the zero grade? If you were to choose to accept the zero grade, you would be making an assumption that the teacher wouldn't accept it. If you chose to not make an assumption by asking the teacher if they would accept the late assignment, you would not be making an assumption. The better route would be to not make the assumption and ask the teacher if they would accept the late assignment. The worse they could say is no.

Ask yourself again, what's the worst that could happen?

By not making an assumption, you are putting yourself closer towards the success you desire. And when you have some wins in this area, you'll be glad you didn't assume the worst. Practice this method every time you are faced with an assumption, and you will see a difference in your life.

FOUR: Have the confidence of a bull

I can tell you first hand that having the right amount of confidence goes a long way in achieving the things you want out of life. Having confidence gives you the ability to seek out and move forward on opportunities, having the effort to try again without backing away, and giving you the self esteem you need to win. Of course, these are just some of the things that confidence allows you to do in your life. In just about anything I do, I display a healthy amount of confidence to achieve the things I want. You must be blinded by what you lack in certain areas to project the level of confidence that people want to see. People love interacting with confident people who can help solve their problems while making their life easier. Confidence breeds success.

FIVE: Stay open minded

It's important to have an open mind as you approach new things in your life. Having a closed mind does no good for you or anyone else, especially if you are trying to overcome an assumption. Having an open mind allows endless opportunities to flow your way. You will start to see several positive outcomes that could happen for you, instead of having a narrow mind; closed off to seeing the opportunity. Keep an open mind and see the opportunities that are in front of you.

SIX: Get additional information to make a sound decision

Many times assumptions are based on a lack of information causing us to make an assumption in the first place. We see this happen when someone makes an assumption towards another person based on very little information. We allow our mind to go down this rabbit hole, thinking that it's ok to do so. What happens is we get stuck in this type of thinking, robbing us of new opportunity. When faced with an assumption, you need to get the additional information needed to take the right step in the right direction.

SEVEN: When in doubt; just ask!

How simple is it that we could just ask a question to get over an assumption we have? While it sounds simple in theory, many people are afraid to ask. That boy at the dance who wants to ask the girl to dance; but doesn't because he assumes she won't like him. Or vice versa. The applicant I mentioned earlier sees a great job opportunity but never applies, because they assume they won't get it. Don't be afraid to ask the right question(s) to get you further towards a positive outcome. It's easier than you think.

I just shared with you how making assumptions can stall you in taking the steps necessary to get the big wins in your life. If you learn to not make assumptions and lean towards getting bigger successes, it will become much easier to win over time.

"It's better to look ahead and prepare, than to look back and regret."

- Jackie Joyner-Kersee

TIME TO LET GO OF THOSE REGRETS

I'm sure at some point everybody has felt some form of regret towards something that has happened in their life, whether it be the current job they hold, or some other event that took place.

Maybe you have some regret about what you're currently doing or have done in the past. Chances are you are reading this book because you are looking to make a change towards a life that is on your own terms, in which case you have made the right choice.

Before we dive further into this topic, let's review what the true definition of regret is.

Regret is an emotion that is focused on the belief that something from the past could have been changed to provide a more desirable outcome. A

type of thinking that imagines your life may have gone differently, if you made a different choice in your past.

Sometimes when I look at my career and the things that I've
worked hard for, I tell myself that I wish I had started earlier in
my life, or that it would have been easier to go after the success
as a younger version of myself, because I would have had less
responsibilities to juggle. If I only changed my life sooner, I would
have had more years to enjoy the fruits of my labor. When having
these thoughts, I remind myself that I probably would not be the
person that I am today without those experiences, good and bad.
Without those past events in my life, I might not be as grateful for
the success I've earned had it been easier for me to attain it.

It can be easy to allow regretful thinking to flood our thoughts,
even with our current success. This is why I feel it's important, and
an absolute must, to let go of any regrets you have so that you
can continue on your path to success. Any regrets that are holding you back should be released into the past and never looked
upon again. If you don't let go of regret and focus more on your
future and what you want to accomplish, you will get stuck on this
sort of carousel going round and round without ever getting anywhere. Regrets can and will stall your journey, if you allow them
to.

Anytime regretful thinking rears its ugly face, I remind myself
of the person I have become as a result of my own journey. The
things that I have achieved were a result of my thinking at that
particular moment. Maybe the drive that I gained to go after my

success would have never happened if I didn't go through those past experiences, or maybe I would not have appreciated the success I earned as much if I had not experienced the hardships that made earning success feel so much better.

Don't regret what you did, or didn't do, so that you can move forward and make your remaining years fruitful and enjoyable. Don't allow yourself to dwell on past incidents that took place, because they don't define who you are at the present moment.

There are many stories of those who went through hardships and came out being a major success. You can find inspiring books on those who chose to curb regretful thinking so that they could design a better life for themselves. You don't have to look far to get inspired by these stories, but you do have to start.

Here are five tips on how you can let go of that regret in your life:

ONE: Give yourself credit that you did your best

Sometimes we can be harder on ourselves than we need to be. When we are forced to think about regret, our thinking will not give us the proper credit we deserve. It will tell you that you could have done better; or you could have made a better choice. Tune out those thoughts and give yourself credit that you got past a regretful time in your life and put your mind at ease.

TWO: Realize the regret was a learning moment

Realize that regret was simply a moment of learning you went through so that you can put it behind you. Just as we should view failures as teaching moments, the same goes for regrets. You learned something from the regret, and then you moved on. Remind yourself of this simple lesson and it will be easier for you to move forward.

THREE: Don't over think about the regret

As I mentioned earlier in this book, it's easy to over think things if we allow our brain to do so. This also applies to regretful thinking. Don't allow yourself to over think, or dwell on the regret(s) you have, because there is nothing you can do about it anyway. Make the decision to move forward and only think about the things that will benefit your journey to a better life.

FOUR: Think of the positives that came from it

While we should be thinking positively all the time, it sure is easier to think negatively. It's easier to complain about how things are, or aren't, instead of taking the time to think of all the positive things. It can be tempting to think you're a bad person because you have regrets floating around in your head, or maybe you aren't deserving of anything positive in your life. When you shift your focus from the negatives to the positives that came from your regret, it can be like a breath of fresh air. No longer will you dwell on those regretful thoughts.

FIVE: Understand that regret is a waste of time

Spending too much time on a regret is a waste of time in itself. Replaying that moment in your life, or thinking of all the negatives, can really keep you in one spot for too long. And we don't need that! Understand that regret is a waste of time and moving on from it will better your current situation. You must live in the present moment.

I'd like to share with you a personal moment from when I was a teenager. I decided one night to leave my parents' home without announcing I was doing so. To avoid going into details, let's just say I was not a fan of the rules that were in place by my parents. I packed all my things in garbage bags and snuck out the window to stay at a friend's house. I spent months living with another friend, sleeping on their couch, landing a low wage job at a local restaurant to stay afloat. I purchased a used car from a buddy of mine, because I had forfeited the nice one that I had when I left home. As you can imagine, this tore a huge hole in my family for that entire time-probably even longer. I eventually came back home after what felt like the longest summer of my life.

I still think about this experience from time to time, wondering if I would have made that same choice again. While my intentions were never to put my family through that emotional roller coaster, it did teach me a very valuable lesson. Leaving my home at such a young age and trying to make it on my own taught me the importance of family. It taught me that my parents had rules in place for a reason and that they were just trying to do right by me, to make sure that I remained safe and respectful. I could look back and dwell on this scenario a million times and think of all the negatives that came from it. Instead, I choose to look at the experience as a lesson that I had to go through, so that I could learn from it and become a better person because of it.

Remember that almost every negative situation has something positive hidden within it. You just have to focus on finding it.

"Today is your day.
Your mountain is
waiting. So get on
your way. "

- Dr. Seuss

DECIDE THAT TODAY IS THE DAY!

TWENTY-THREE

Back in 1587, Sir Francis Bacon said something that has been shared countless times, *"Knowledge itself is power"*. While this is a great quote that will stand the test of time. I don't believe it to be 100% true. Knowledge in itself is power, but it must be followed by action. You could read this book, or any other relatable information on what you're doing, but it won't do you any good unless you take the necessary actions to change your life.

If you combine everything you've learned with the action steps to achieve what you want out of life, you can become a powerful force for good. You will see your life begin to change for the better. By building your skills and becoming an expert in your chosen area of interest, while taking the necessary steps towards hitting your goal(s), you can really create the life you want You will have beaten the *force of average!* Just like a soldier preparing for war, you will have armed yourself with the knowledge needed to win at whatever opportunity you go after. You will beat your competition and most importantly, the past version of yourself.

I shared with you the importance of self education and how you should always be a student of learning. By learning and applying your action steps, you will make the decision to go after success on a daily basis. You will no longer allow yourself to make excuses, telling yourself to not do something. You will be a knowledgeable person of action!

Here are 4 tips to help you decide today is the day to get started:

ONE: Decide what you want and take the first step

When you decide on what you want for your life, it's time to take the first step. By figuring out what this first step is for yourself, you will be able to get going; today. This could mean you start applying for a better job, or you finally start that business you've been thinking about. Maybe it means you could take a night class to further your education to increase your skill set. Decide what you want to do and take the first step.

TWO: Every day add another step

Once you have taken that first step, it's time to add another step;

day after day. Taking additional steps will gradually get you to where you want to be, taking multiple steps daily towards your goal(s). These steps could be big or small, provided that you are actually adding steps to your daily routine. The more you commit to this, the easier it will be because it will become a habitual routine.

THREE: Write down your action steps

When you figure out what you want to do, it's time to write down your daily steps so you can implement them without over thinking, or procrastinating People who follow a plan will have a better chance of succeeding versus those who try to 'wing it'. Once you've written down your steps, simply follow your plan. You can accomplish this through the use of a daily planner to keep you on track. Don't ever stray from your plan either. There will be times where you will need to adjust some things as you go about your day, week, or month. But you need to have a plan in place if you want to succeed.

FOUR: Know that progress takes patience

You may begin to feel like you aren't getting anywhere, even after you have taken your daily action steps. This is considered normal, because progress and change takes time. It may also mean you need to revise what steps you are taking over the course of your journey as you learn what works and what doesn't work for you. Your action steps need to be reviewed daily in an effort to ensure they are working for you. The road to success is never a smooth path, because it's always under construction. You must be willing to adjust what steps you are taking daily towards creating your new life. Don't be afraid to change it up either. Real change doesn't happen overnight.

You just learned not only the importance of getting started on your new life, but you have also learned that taking that first step is crucial to making things happen for yourself. If you don't take the first step towards greatness, then you will remain where you are currently at, under the *force of average*.

"It's time to start living the life you've imagined."

- Henry James

IT'S YOUR LIFE, SO START LIVING IT

One of the best lessons I've learned in my life is that I own my life, no matter what happens to me. I make the choice of who I let in, or keep in my circle of friends, or even family. I am the only one responsible for the things in my life that need changing. I am the only one responsible for creating the life I want to live. Nobody else. I am the creator of my destiny and I own that responsibility; happily.

It's amazing to me how some people share the complaints of their life with others, as if they are not responsible for their own actions, or how their life played out. They spew out how unlucky they are and how life has dealt them a bad hand. I'm not talking about those who are actually dealing with a tragic situation that they can't change or improve. I'm referring to the complainers who share their drama with anyone who lends an ear. Those who whine about how much their life sucks and how it would be so much better if certain people would make better choices. The whiners who blame a company for paying so little, yet they accept the pay without ever making themselves worth more to the company or marketplace.

I guess these people find it easier to complain about things than to change their behavior and habits behind it. If only these people took the initiative to take charge of their life and live it on their own terms, trading complaints for positive actions. I can't tell you how empowering it is to own your life-and act accordingly.

This is not to say that a complaint or two doesn't slip out of my mouth from time to time. I consider myself a work in progress. The difference between someone who owns their life and someone who doesn't is that people who own their life don't stay in that position of complaining for long, they move on from the negative chatter and take charge of their life. Meanwhile the complainers continue on that path for the rest of their life without getting anywhere. And they will try to drag down those around them in the process.

Here are six tips to living life on your terms:

ONE: Remind yourself that it's your life

Who is in charge of your life? You are! You are the only person who is in charge of your life and how you choose to live it. Your friends, family or even spouse do not rule how you live your life. You are the master of your thinking and actions and it's up to you to live life on your own terms. When you are falling into the trap of complaining a lot, remind yourself that you are in charge of your current life and where it's headed in the future.

TWO: It's up to you to find happiness

While it certainly helps to hang around other happy people, it's up to you to make yourself happy. You should never rely on some-one else to create happiness for you. I know this sounds harsh, but it's the best thing you can do for yourself. You must find things in your life that make you happy, so that you can be a better person to those around you. If you come home grumpy from a job you hate and are a terror to those around you, are you really helping anyone else? You are no good to anyone if you are constantly miserable and lacking internal happiness.

THREE: Don't keep waiting for things to happen

Do you feel like you hate your job, yet you aren't applying for other opportunities? Maybe some people you know have gotten a better job, or promotion, and you haven't asked them how they did it. Now is the time to stop procrastinating and get after what you want and rid yourself of what you hate. Don't keep waiting for someone or something else to make it better for you, discover what the change is and move towards it.

FOUR: Make the most of your time

Often what humans get wrong about life is that they assume that they have all the time in the world left to do what they want. We live our life thinking we have much more life available to accomplish the things we want. The problem with this thinking is that our future is never guaranteed. Of course this sounds grim, but it's the reality of life. Something could happen in life that could cause us to not have that future time we thought we had. Make the most of your time by ridding your life of things, or people, that waste your time, allowing you to live life to the fullest.

FIVE: Conquer that stress

Having too much stress could rob you of having great opportunities, better days, causing you to stumble or feel overwhelmed with something or someone. Taking the time to conquer your stress can also help you live a better life, one with calmness, tranquility and smoother days. You can conquer your stress by exercising, cutting back on bad food choices, or even taking on a hobby of interest. Find something that brings your stress level down and incorporate that into your routine.

SIX: Implement the 'One-Month Rule'

Grab a notepad and quickly write down three things you've wanted to achieve. This could be getting a new job, saving a specified amount of money, or even something as simple as organizing the items in your kitchen cabinets. Set a deadline of one month to complete each task and get it done. Set a calendar alert as your deadline. The late Napolean Hill once said "A goal is a dream *with a deadline."* This is true for your life as well.

You just read six tips on how you can take ownership of your life. Never allow yourself to be that complainer, or person who does nothing to take charge of their life. It will be your decision that helps you create the life you want to live. Keep these tips in front of you and apply them daily.

"A candle loses nothing by lighting another candle"

- James Keller

SUCCESSFUL PEOPLE SHARE THEIR STORIES

There is a great quote by Author James Keller that goes *"A candle loses nothing by lighting another candle."* Which is why I would like to share with you the success stories of others who have changed their mindset and achieved the life they truly want to live. These are people who have beaten the *force of average* to live a life they truly look forward to.

Here are their stories:

Herby Fabius is an entrepreneur founder of Billion Success Media, an online platform that encourages entrepreneurs and authors to teach others by sharing success stories and lessons learned from real-life experiences. Herby is a self-published author, who has published three business books. Including Business Lessons: 150+ Startup Mistakes and Entrepreneurship

Lessons Shared by 55 Successful Founders. Billion Success Media is a support system to help new entrepreneurs and authors start their passion businesses. They offer Web Design services and web maintenance support to new authors and entrepreneurs with Billion Hosting.

Jason Gelios: When was it that you decided to do something differently and/or take a new direction in your life or work?

Herby Fasius: I always wanted to have my own online business. I tried a lot of different things, but none worked out. I co-founded tech companies and even had side hustles offering web design services on the side.

I did it for as long as I could, but then I went to work in corporate. Over the years, I slowly lost the passion I had for building my own business. I was too comfortable at my corporate job, so it seemed like I didn't have to take a risk on starting my own business.

But, just like many others, I was let go from my corporate job because of Covid-19. It was not easy finding a job. Luckily for me, I kept all my sites up and running. I never took them down, so I just pick up where I left off. I decided to take skills and experience into a different direction.

I realized, being an employee is very similar to being an entrepreneur. In order to get a job, you must have a resume and more importantly, you have to be able to convince someone to take a chance on you. Well, it's pretty much the same with building a new business. You have to build your reputation (Resume) and then you must go out and convince customers to take a chance on you to buy your products/services.

Jason Gelios: What's the biggest factor that has helped you be successful?

Herby Fasius: One of the biggest things that have helped me to be where I am today s my ability to take risks and not worry too much about the outcome. There have been plenty of times in my life where I have second-guessed my decision-making. Fortunately, for me, I am always able to convince myself to try things, even when the odds are against me. We are all afraid of the unknown, therefore we're afraid of taking a little bit of risk. Becoming successful at anything in this life comes with a price – we all have to pay.

Jason Gelios: What are your success habits?

Herby Fasius: Being productive is one of the most important things for entrepreneurs. With so much to do and so little time, it is important we use our time wisely.

With that said, I have two habits that have worked for me when it comes to productivity.

Planning tomorrow the night before.

Every day before bed I make a list of the most important things that I must complete the next day. This is crucial for me. If I skip this step and accidently go to bed without making a list – I can almost guarantee nothing will get done the next day. (Believe me, I have tested it many times.)

Get The One Thing Done.

As I mentioned, I plan my day the night before, however, I understand that not everything on the list is going to get done. So, at the top of my list is The One Thing that must be done (I focus on getting the One Thing Done first.) Over the years, I have learned that the hard things (the things I don't like to do) are usually the most important things. So, I make sure to get the one thing done. That way if I get nothing else completed, my day is not a complete loss.

Jason Gelios: What mistakes have you made along the way?

Herby Fasius: I have made a lot of mistakes. The first book I ever published was a compilation of all the mistakes I and others have made at the beginning of our entrepreneurship careers. "Business Lessons" was a suitable topic for me, because there were so many things I wish I had done differently in the beginning.

Here are two examples:

I would not have let FEAR slow my progress

FEAR has always been an issue with me. There are things that I wanted to try in the past that I never got to do, because I was afraid it wasn't going to work. The FEAR of judgment from others was also another factor. It wasn't until I learned not to care much that things started changing. We all have FEAR, but the key is to not let FEAR make our decisions for us. Do not make decisions based on FEAR.

I was not consistent enough

I took a break from my work. Because of it, I ended up wasting a lot of time. A couple of years ago things seemed like they were staying still and not moving fast enough, so I decided to take a couple of months off. This turned into almost 3 years. Now, I can only think of how much I could have accomplished in those 3 years, if I didn't take a break.

Jason Gelios: What personal challenges have you overcome to stay the course?

Herby Fasius: There have been many personal challenges along the way, but I have managed to keep moving forward. Over the years, I have learned that business is a marathon, not a sprint. No matter how tough it gets, I always remind myself that as long as I keep moving forward one step at a time, eventually, I will get to my destination. Always keep in mind, small steps are better than no steps.

Jason Gelios: What is the best advice you can give someone looking to make a positive change in their life and beat the *force of average*?

Herby Fasius: I am always a bit reluctant to giving advice to others, because everyone has their own path. When it comes to business, or even making a positive change, it takes a lot of effort, dedication, and consistency. What worked for me, might not work for you. Instead of giving you advice, I am going to share three things I wish I did at the beginning of my journey and, hopefully, it can help you.

1 – Consistency is key. It doesn't matter what your goal is, the only way you will get there is by staying consistent day in, day out. There are absolutely no days off. You must stay consistent at all costs. The best way to think of this is...let's say you're building a 10-story building. You must first focus on laying the first brick, then continue to lay bricks every single day. Do not focus on how much work it will take to build a 10-story building. You simply, focus on laying each brick as perfect as you can and continue to do so on a daily basis, and before you know it, you'll soon have your 10-story building.

2 – Give it time. Everything takes time to build. Most people fail because they had an unrealistic expectation of the amount of time it will take to build what they're trying to create. Give it time to grow. This also falls in line with being consistent. You have to be able to stay the course for a very long time to see it become a success.

<><><><><><><><><><><><><><><><><><><><><><>

Peter Mason is an entrepreneur and the President of ExtriCARE USA, an innovative medical device company distributing the Extri-

CARE product line nationally to the USA and Canada. With over 10 years of experience in strategic business development and sales, Peter utilizes his skills to help expand the ExtriCARE product line to revolutionize and lead the direction of Negative Pressure Wound Therapy (NPWT) worldwide.

Peter grew up in a small town in Maine, with a father an accredited medical doctor (D.O.) and mother a registered nurse. Because of his parents' involvement in the medical space, he has always been interested in it. His professional career started in 2008 upon graduation from Temple University. Over his professional career, he has owned or been involved in many startup companies ranging from video production to IT services. He also has a background in theater where he has worked as an Actor on a small budget to feature films. Peter was introduced to NPWT in 2012 during his time at a medical manufacturer with the role of sales manager and business development.

Peter strongly believes the NPWT market is still in its infancy stage and will have tremendous growth in the coming years. He hopes to continue innovating and producing a cost effective product line that will shape and transform NPWT, helping wounds heal much more efficiently.

Jason Gelios: When was it that you decided to do something differently / take a new direction in your life or work?

Peter Mason: I can tell you it was not something that happened overnight. For perspective, let me start with a bit of my background, which I feel is important because there is not a straight or perfect path—it is something you need to cultivate and build upon with an ever-evolving plan. In my experience, very rarely does the original plan stay the course "perfectly". Don't get me wrong, planning is important, but I try to focus on the goal and less about the plan, because oftentimes opportunities come along the way that you may miss if you are too focused on executing your plan. Sometimes you need to detour and that detour maybe what gets you to an even better place.

When I graduated college, I took a job in admissions for a private boarding school. I took the job, because the position was remote and allowed me to travel to schools around the country. It was a great job, but something felt missing and I needed to pursue something I was truly passionate about. However, I was comfortable and made enough money to pay the bills and have a bit of fun. So, I saved as much as I could and I knew down deep that I needed to keep moving. I quit my comfortable job and bought a motorcycle. Then, I proceeded to zig zag 10,000 miles across the country. I drove for two months driving down most of the west coast and then worked my way back to the east coast. During this not so comfortable motorcycle journey, I had a lot of time to think.

To think about what motivated me and how I wanted to spend my time on this earth. I knew after this trip I wanted to make an impact and I realized how fast money can come and go. I also knew I wanted control over my future and needed to be a sponge and learn more of how I could achieve this control. I knew I had to build my experience and started interviewing jobs in sales. I landed on an entry level 9am to 5pm sales job for a medical man-ufacturer.

Now this was not easy and during my first year there were many days I wanted to give up, however, I knew if I could learn how to be-come important to the company and rise up, that I could learn how to run my own company, or at the very least use those skills at other companies to be effective. I found a great mentor in this company that helped me learn the skills like the art of deal in negotiation and how to listen. After working up to national sales manager and working 5 yrs, there was still a lot missing. This is another point when I realized I needed to do something different and wanted that control of my time and life.

Jason Gelios: What's the biggest factor that has helped you be successful?

Peter Mason: The biggest factors that have helped me be success-ful have come from skills I have developed. The great thing about skills is you can improve them by practicing them.

The first and foremost skill necessary to be a successful entre-preneur is to have emotional intelligence (EI). This is important in business and leadership, because it serves as a vessel to help you navigate challenges and successes. A good entrepreneur is someone who makes connections and builds trust with the peo-ple they connect with. When you have emotional intelligence, you are more set up to help others effectively, which in turn will also help you. I believe EI is something that you can develop and practice, which can be increased over time. One can practice it by learning the art of effective and active communication. Listen more and focus on what others are saying, rather than what you want to say.

The second skill is having the ability to problem solve and not get discouraged by roadblocks. Successful people use failure as a tool to learn and grow—they fail forward. If you focus too much on what didn't go right, you lose focus on moving forward towards your goals and vision. Be solution-oriented during failure and use it to pivot, adapt and move forward.

The last skill is to be creative. Part of being savvy is finding ways to differentiate yourself from the rest. Having a creative spirit allows you to cultivate the confidence to challenge the status quo. Develop the ability to think outside the box and find creative solutions when it's not right in front of you.

In general, take risks and get out of your comfort zone.

Jason Gelios: What are your success habits?

Peter Mason: Don't Settle – You have one life, live it to its fullest potential. If you want something, fight for it.

- Keep evolving and Learning
- Don't fear failure
- Not a race. Sometimes it's the long game that wins. No matter how overwhelming it seems, start by focusing on one step at a time.
- "Moving the needle"

Jason Gelios: What mistakes have you made along the way?

Peter Mason: Well, none! To me, it is only a mistake if you do not learn something from what went wrong and you change and adapt to avoid repeating that "mistake" in the future. If I looked at this any other way, then there would be too many mistakes to list!

I believe mistakes have a negative connotation in our culture, and that needs change. Mistakes are important to learning what not to do and I feel a lot of people don't attempt to act out of fear of making a mistake. So, our mindset needs to change to a more positive perspective regarding mistakes. Let's be mindful when we make a mistake and think about what we can do to avoid that situation in the future or what we need to learn from that situation so we can evolve ourselves to be better and grow.

A time in my life when I needed to learn from a mistake was when I took on more than I could chew. At one point, I was working a full-time sales job and trying to get two different startup companies off the ground. I was running around like a chicken with my head cut off. I thought being an entrepreneur meant seizing every opportunity that came my way and trying to do it all. My eagerness and desire to do everything clouded my judgment on what I thought I could do vs. what I could actually do. The result of all my time was a lot of frustration and the launch failure of both startup companies. However, I learned many valuable lessons from this time in my life.

Jason Gelios: What personal challenges have you overcome to stay the course?

Peter Mason: At a young age, I was diagnosed with dyslexia, which is a learning disorder that makes it difficult to read and learn in the traditional sense. Having to overcome and find ways to deal with this has given me patience and forced me to find ways to do things differently. Having dyslexia is out of my control, but finding ways to adapt is completely in my control. Knowing what I struggle with and finding solutions, or someone who can help, has helped me a lot as an entrepreneur. In business, I've learned that it is very important and one of the best things I can do is surround myself with people that have strengths where I am weak.

Jason Gelios: What is the best advice you can give someone looking to make a positive change in their life and beat the *force of average*?

Peter Mason: Like many that desire a life change, I started with reading books, searching for what other entrepreneurs have done through the web and finding people who were doing things I would want to do and attempting to connect with them.

I highly encourage finding or having a mentor that has success in the areas you want to learn about and thrive in.

If you have a passion, start there. Find ways to turn that passion into a business or lifestyle.

If you think you can offer something innovative, or better than the status quo, start by putting your ideas together and developing a simple action plan. Take one step at a time and if you get overwhelmed, try focusing on one item on your list and completing that item and then focus on the next one. When I get overwhelmed, I focus on the whole list and everything I need to do and end up not getting anything done.

In general, take risks and get out of your comfort zone. In my experience, this is where I have grown the most. Most importantly, be open to constantly learning whenever you can.

<><><><><><><><><><><><><><><><><><><><>

Earl L. Jones is an nsurance agency owner located in the San Francisco Bay Area. He works with local business, home owners, and individuals with their insurance needs. In addition, he also has a mobile notary business as well. He also teaches group fitness and fundraises for a local charity. He's now serving on a local board of directors for a not-profit charity for the homeless.

Jason Gelios: When was it that you decided to do something differently / take a new direction in your life or work?

Earl Jones: I decided this as a kid. I grew up on the North Side in St. Louis, MO. I saw my share of poverty, crime, etc. I also saw love, support, and encouragement. I was constantly told to get an education and get out of the neighborhood.

Jason Gelios: What's the biggest factor that has helped you be successful?

Earl Jones: There are so many factors. One, my mom raised 3 kids as a single mom. When she met my step-dad, he made it his mission to provide for his family. They did not tolerate low academic performance of any kind. Two, It was also being exposed to different races and cultures. I was part of the desegregation school program. That exposed me to not only white people, it also espoused me to people of color that were middle class.

Jason Gelios: What are your success habits?

Earl Jones: It's personal growth and development. It's taking seminars, reading books, and taking actions on the information. It's learning to only say yes to those things and people that are in alignment with my vision. Its adopting quickly. It's realizing that I can't do everything... so asking for help and support from the right people. Yes, I can say systems, but if the foundation isn't right, then systems can only take you so far. Look at Blockbuster.

Jason Gelios: What mistakes have you made along the way?

Earl Jones: I've made my share. I chose to ignore the advice of my mentor, State Farm Agent, Joe Trapasso. He told me how to handle my former district manager and his boss at State Farm during my 1st year. I didn't listen and it cost me my agency. They told me I wasn't good enough to play in the sandbox... despite the fact I was out performing agents with decades of experience. And despite the fact that "I'm loved and respected." I've since learned, when your mentor says "jump", you jump. There are people out here that claim to mean well, yet every conversation is about what you aren't doing. Learn to tell those people to kick rocks.

Jason Gelios: What personal challenges have you overcome to stay the course?

Earl Jones: Belief in myself. I've been knocked down a few times. I've lost money. I've been told I'm not good enough. That stuff plays with your mind and faith. So some days, it's literally just getting out of bed and get back to it. It's getting back up to fight when there's blood in your eyes.

Jason Gelios: What is the best advice you can give someone looking to make a positive change in their life and beat the force of average?

Earl Jones: Invest in your personal growth and development. The biggest battle to achieve any success lies between your two ears.

<><><><><><><><><><><><><><><><><>

Ryan Balicki is the owner of Copper Hop Brewing Company in Southeast Michigan. To share a little bit about Ryan, he was in Corporate America for about 20 years, before he decided to venture off and start his own business. Ryan had done real estate for about 4-5 years prior to that to kind of figure out what running your own business is like on a smaller scale, without really having to worry about somebody else working for you, or people relying on you like his current day to day responsibilities. That gave Ryan a little insight on what type of internal motivation you need in order to push forward and do something on your own.

Jason Gelios: When was it that you decided to do something different and take a new direction in your life or work?

Ryan Balicki: I think I knew around the age of 35-36, being 41 at the time of this interview, that every company I worked for I was making somebody else a lot of money. Sure I made good money as well, but I was like, 'why am I working this hard for other people, when I can be working this hard for myself?' I guess that was my eureka moment. I have a lot of knowledge in a lot of different things and I think I could apply what I've learned the last 15-16 years of my life into opening up something for myself. That was probably the moment that I decided I'm going to do this. I'm going to figure it out.

Jason Gelios: What was the biggest factor that helped you be successful?

Ryan Balicki: I think it's the ability to not be afraid to ask questions that you don't know the answers to. A lot of people want to seem like they know everything, so they typically are afraid to ask somebody else a question. Getting into the brewery world, there was a lot I didn't know about it. I had to go out and visit another brewery to converse with the owner, while drinking their beer, to figure out how they did certain things, or what they did right. Those conversations helped immensely with making sure that I was building a proper foundation for my company before it even opened.

I think probably one of the bigger factors, was getting out there and really just learning as much about what I was about to go do myself, without being afraid to ask some questions, even some tougher questions that were maybe uncomfortable to ask and answer. It needed to be done.

Jason Gelios: What are your success habits?

Ryan Balicki: I do a lot of voice memos, recordings and setting reminders on my phone. I think probably one of the best books I read that helped me with this was 'The One Thing' by Gary Keller. I used to be a big multitasker, although there really is no such thing as multitasking. You either are focusing on one thing, or you're not. If you focus on more than one thing, then you're just taking longer to do things. So the book really focuses on prioritizing things and then getting them done one by one. That has been helpful for me, because I prioritize my list of things to do daily, then I'll tackle the toughest or most important one first, continuing to tackle the rest. You might not be able to get them all done, so you move them to the next day. I think that was huge for me to help with my success.

Jason Gelios: What mistakes have you made along the way you?

Ryan Balicki: To me, mistakes are learning opportunities in my opinion. I don't know if there are any huge mistakes that I've made along the way. I would say one of the biggest issues I have is that when there's something that needs to change drastically, I sometimes drag my feet, because I don't like making those drastic changes where you might need to adapt quickly to it. An example of this is the Covid-19 pandemic. We were regulated by the state and couldn't serve our guests inside. We had a small outside patio with all these opportunities for us to do outside seating, but we couldn't really do it in an area that I felt was good enough for our staff and customers. There was a spot that I wanted to really do it in, but it wasn't as easy as just making it happen there, because we didn't own the property. I know this question was supposed to be about mistakes, but I think in that particular situation, I could have done something sooner, instead I chose to wait a little bit and do it the way I wanted to do it. It did take a little longer than I wanted it to, but that's ok.

Some of the biggest mistakes that I make are not jumping on certain things right away, because I like to look at the longevity or the bigger picture of things. I guess I kind of made this question turn into why I do something the way I do it, but I'll be honest, I don't think we have made a ton of mistakes along the way. Any mistakes we made turned into a great learning experience and I think we've done pretty well.

Jason Gelios: What personal challenges have you overcome to stay the course?

Ryan Balicki: I think the biggest personal challenge, when you're opening your own business, is work-life balance. This is especially true if you have a family. For me it's a wife, four kids, a lot of demands at home, and at the time, a business that was a baby in a sense that needed a lot more time and nurturing than even my own family did when it first opened. Luckily, we were able to overcome me having to be there all day everyday rather quickly. But that was probably the biggest personal challenge of me being used to being home every night for dinner and putting the kids to bed. When you open your own business, you sacrifice that time you used to spend elsewhere; but for good reason. It feels great to really put in the necessary time to want what you're doing to be successful long term.

Jason Gelios: What is the best advice you can give someone looking to make a positive change in their life and beat the *force of average*?

Ryan Balicki: Don't just jump into something to make the change. Do your research and figure out a game plan. My business plan that I made was over 80 pages. I had multiple people tell me it was the most in-depth business plan that they had ever seen. I'll be honest, I didn't reinvent the wheel. I simply took a new business plan that had a layout from another business and I looked at what they did and put my information in. I did all the research needed to turn that blue print, or that format, into a business plan that answered all those questions for my business. There were things that I took out and items I added into the plan.

You don't have to jump right into a huge change, because you can do your research and figure out why you're doing it first. Definitely make sure it's something you want to do, because I think a lot of people make changes in their life because of monetary reasons, instead of basing their decision on what really makes them happy-which might not be money. Figure out what your motivator is and what makes you happy when it comes to work. Is it working for you? Is it money? Is it recognition? All those things are important in figuring out what you want to do.

I will tell you that my little brother really was all about how he could just make money quickly. He wanted to make a lot of money and do all these things. But outside of that drive to make money, he was really big into personal fitness and had a love for people and helping them in general. I told him maybe you're meant to go the fitness route and become a personal trainer to help people with their fitness and health goals. My brother decided to pursue that path and he succeeded in that aspect, because that was where his passion was outside of work. His passion was health and fitness.

Look at yourself and figure out what you like to do. I very much enjoyed craft beer and even just talking to people and having those conversations. For me, that's ultimately why I chose to open up a brewery. Find what one thing you do now that you love in life, and see if there's a way that you can make a career out of that. Every day will seem like work now, but I'll be honest, there's a ton of stuff you got to do even with those jobs when you own your own business. You can't avoid that.

As you have just read from these successful professionals, they didn't always have the success they currently have. It was through a change in their mindset and learning how to navigate through the tough times they experienced that got them to where they are today. When we learn how others have had similar struggles in pursuit of greatness, it can give us the hope we need to get there as well, achieving the goals we set for ourselves.

Feel free to revisit these success stories when you are in need of inspiration and guidance in your own life. You can also go one step further and follow these people on their social media platforms.

I invite you to keep this book close and reference it as you begin your journey towards your new life; one of your choosing. A life that you created for yourself, that you don't mind living.

If you found value in this read, please leave a review. You can also share your story of success by visiting www.jasongelios.com and click on the 'book' page. I would love to hear how you overcame the *force of average*! Please share this book with others who would like to beat the *force of average* in their own lives.

Now go out there, beat the force of average, and change your life for the better!

ABOUT THE AUTHOR
Jason Gelios

TOP PRODUCING REALTOR

Jason is a top producing REALTOR serving the Southeast Michigan market and surrounding areas. Jason works with home buyers, sellers, and investors to help accomplish their goals of buying, selling, or leasing real estate. Jason approaches every client with his 'client for life' philosophy to help them achieve their real estate goals.

EXPERT MEDIA CONTRIBUTOR

Jason is sourced across the globe for his real estate expertise to the likes of Fox Business, Yahoo Money, Realtor.com, Best Company, The Mortgage Reports, GoBankingRates, BobVila.com and more. Jason has also been interviewed by publications such as Authority Magazine, Buzzfeed, Billion Success, The Human Resolve, Ticker News, Thrive Global and more for his life changing success tips that he has learned and implemented in his own life.

AUTHOR
As you learned, Jason is the author of this book '**Beating The Force Of Average**'. He is also the author of the real estate book '**Think Like a Realtor**. A book about the buying and selling of residential real estate' where he shares his real world situations and expertise that could save readers thousands of dollars.

REAL ESTATE BLOGGER
Jason shares articles on various topics from home owner tips, life changing advice, and expertise on buying and selling real estate through h s popular blog.
Visit www.ItsAllAboutTheRealEstate.com/jasons-blog.

PUBLIC SPEAKER
Jason delivers valuab.e home buying knowledge through home buying seminars, tapping into his expertise and real world experiences in real estate, benefitting home buyers.

CREATOR AND HOST OF THE ASKJASONGELIOS SHOW
Creator and Host of *The AskJasonGelios Real Estate Show*, Jason educates viewers on various topics ranging from buying and selling residential real estate to home owner tips, providing valueable information on a weekly basis.

MONTHLY E-NEWSLETTER
Jasons monthly e-newsletter, Happy Living Digest, shares tips on home buying and selling, as well as helpful home maintenance and seasonal how to projects.
Subscribe for free at www.ItsAllAboutTheRealEstate.com!

CONNECT WITH JASON

JASON'S WEBSITES
www.ItsAllAboutTheRealEstate.com
www.JasonGelios.com

REAL ESTATE BLOG
www.ItsAllAboutTheRealEstate.com/jasons-blog

YOUTUBE
Search 'Jason Gelios' or visit the link
https://www.youtube.com/c/ItsAllAboutTheRealEstate

FACEBOOK
https://www.facebook.com/jasongeliosrealtor/

TWITTER
https://twitter.com/jasongelios

INSTAGRAM
https://www.instagram.com/jasongeliosrealtor/

PINTEREST
https://www.pinterest.com/jasongelios/

LINKEDIN
https://www.linkedin.com/in/jasongelios/